INTRODUCTION

The original purpose of these writings was catharsis. At first, it was just that, cathartic. But, after more than twenty years of marriage to a man who was diagnosed by two psychiatrists to have a "severe narcissistic personality disorder" had done inestimable damage. The aching, painful loneliness, self-recrimination, constant and pervasive fear, endless self-examination, self-doubt and self-blame accompanied by a loss of self, struggling to resist normalizing unhealthy behaviors and the continuous failure to do so, etc. did the same.

Then one wise woman suggested that it might be helpful to provide information to others who are involved in and/or considering long term involvement with someone who has narcissistic personality disorder. That opened the option to partially make the whole awful thing mean something and perhaps some good could come from it.

The third significant factor came in a very unexpected form. The enormous coverage of the Trump campaign

From the beginning I was fully aware that in describing this very unhappy and destructive marriage, it would appear that I was pointing fingers, laying blame, whining, etc. But the very value of these writings rests in pointing out and describing the ramifications of being closely involved with a person who has Narcissistic Personality Disorder. The goal therefore, is to point out the "red flags", the indicators, and offer ways to make wise and positive decisions. So, here I invoke a mantra I developed using it as a "shield" when his raging and rants began.

"He is not mean, he is not bad; his disordered world is all he has. He's doing his best; his best is not something I can detest." It did not solve problems, but it did deter escalation of them.

My own deeply beloved daughter recently shouted at me ACCUSINGLY "You have serious mental health issues, Mom." I had been aware of that for several years, was pained by it and the effects it had on her; had done everything I could to alleviate the damage: therapy, hypnosis, self-hypnosis, smoking, support groups, medication, even turned to alcohol for about 2 years, neurokinesis,etc.. They all gave some temporary relief, but none were lasting or satisfying. PTSD is at least as painful for the sufferer as for those around them, probably much more. More than twenty years of serious, destructive discord would not be undone easily if at all. I had always believed I would get support from her. That was my last hope for help. All I had left was my faith and I believe it will be adequate support. Friends had helped but most truly felt and/or said, "get over it, move on". Well intentioned, but, SO inadequate.

After the marriage ended, and far too late I did a great deal more research on narcissistic personality disorder, read approximately forty-six books on the subject, some good, some not as good, but none provided me the information, vocabulary, and style of delivery that would have helped me when I most needed it. I'm putting together a book I wish I had had so long ago.

At the end of this treatise is a list with short descriptions of the symptoms of Narcissistic Personality Disorder. Please do not focus on the more commonly known concept of *narcissism*. Instead, for clarity, focus on the **<u>disordered</u>** personality aspect. In addition, it is helpful to remember that a person with narcissistic personality disorder is more than the disorder. Each will have their own assets, liabilities, and distinguishing characteristics. Summarily, this work will focus on the evolution of the relationship as well as the slow and very painful realization described above providing the reader with:

1. Initial narratives depicting real life experience with someone with serious NPD. Hopefully, this will allow one to begin to identify with, recognize and determine the type and seriousness which they may or may not be dealing with;

2. The second part will be a summary of what I have learned from my experience, research, skilled therapists, and years of reflection, prayer and some very caring people;

3. The last, because it is a current, public and dramatic depiction of almost all the symptoms of NPD as they are

acted out by Trump, a classic example of severe (in his case possibly malignant) NPD. Some helpful concepts and phrases have assisted me to put into words the chaos and confusion I had been trying to discern for years. I hope they will be helpful to those reading this book.

While it was enormously helpful to see the symptoms of NPD so dramatically portrayed during the campaign for the presidency and since, it was also devastating and humiliating to watch Sean Spicer, Sandra Sanders and others who acted as press secretaries representing DT grow into practiced, accomplished liars, recognizing that this was what I had allowed to happen to me.

<u>FOREWARD</u>

Personality Disorders are a class of mental disorders characterized by maladaptive patterns of behavior, cognitive and inner experience exhibited across many contexts and deviating markedly from those accepted by the individual's culture. These patterns develop early, are inflexible, and are associated with significant distress or disability.

"Narcissistic Personality Disorder (NPD) is a serious condition which affects an estimated 1% of the population. Narcissism is characterized by an **<u>extreme</u>** self-interest and promotion with an accompanying lack of concern for the needs of others".

American Psychiatric Association, DSM 5 2015

As my own awareness and knowledge of this illness has grown. I believe we will learn that the percentage is far higher.

The combination of narcissism and a personality disorder is divisive, destructive, DANGEROUS, incurable and abusive.

American Psychiatric Association, DSM 5 2015

Those with personality disorders typically engage in antisocial behaviors, maladaptive behaviors in relationships that ultimately exploit, demean, and hurt their intimate partners, family members and friends.

They use a plethora of diversionary tactics to distort the reality of their victims and deflect responsibility. Although those who are not narcissistic can employ these tactics as well; abusive narcissists use them to excess in an effort to escape accountability for their actions.

There are many descriptions of personality disorder. This is an amalgamation of some of them.

If one has narcissistic personality disorder, they may come across as conceited, boastful, arrogant or pretentious. You often monopolize conversations, may belittle or look down on people you perceive as inferior. You may feel a sense of entitlement — and when you don't receive special treatment, you may become impatient or angry. You may insist on having "the best" of everything — for instance, the best car, athletic club or medical care.

At the same time, they have great trouble handling anything that may be **perceived** as criticism. You may have secret feelings of insecurity, shame, vulnerability and humiliation. To feel better, you may react with rage or contempt and try to belittle the other person to make yourself appear superior. Or you may feel **victimized**, depressed and moody because you fall short of perfection.

Many experts use the criteria in the Diagnostic and Statistical Manual of Mental Disorders (DSM-5), published by the American Psychiatric Association, to diagnose mental conditions.

DSM-5 criteria for narcissistic personality disorder (NPD) include these features:

- Having an exaggerated sense of self-importance
- Expecting to be recognized as superior even without achievements that warrant it
- Exaggerating your achievements and talents
  - Being preoccupied with fantasies about success, power, brilliance, beauty or the perfect mate
  - Believing that you are superior and can only be understood by or associate with equally <u>special people</u>
  - Requiring constant admiration
  - Having a sense of entitlement
  - Expecting special favors and unquestioning compliance with your expectations
  - Taking advantage of others to get what you want
  - Having an inability or unwillingness to recognize the needs and feelings of others

- Being envious of others and believing others envy you
- Behaving in an arrogant or haughty manner

Although some features of narcissistic personality disorder may seem like having confidence, it's far from the same. Narcissistic personality disorder crosses the border of healthy confidence into thinking so highly of yourself that you put yourself on a <u>pedestal</u> and value yourself far more than you value others.

When you have narcissistic personality disorder, you may not want to think that anything could be wrong — <u>in fact the NEED to see yourself as flawless is inherent in and an integral necessity for the person to survive.</u> People with narcissistic personality disorder are most likely to <u>seek treatment</u> when they develop <u>symptoms of depression</u> — often because of perceived criticisms or rejections.

There are levels of Narcissistic Personality Disorder (NPD) but some disagreement among mental health professionals about the specific behaviors associated with each level. Briefly the levels from least serious to most: Serious NPD, Severe NPD, and Malignant NPD.

TABLE OF CONTENTS

INTRODUCTION

SECTION 2

<u>AND SO, IT BEGAN</u>

They were there! THE RED FLAGS,… waving, flashing, glaring Red Flags, caution signs, warnings. But where was I? Was I blindly in love, overwhelmed by significant demands, submerged in my own neurotic caretaker role, was it arrogance? I am a trained, experienced psychiatric social worker and should have known better. If this could happen to me, with my training as a certified psychiatric social worker, how much more disorienting and harmful would it be for someone with no related training?

I met Dennis in late September of 1975 while on a date with another man. My date had hopes of starting his own business and had been given Dennis's name as someone with whom he might want to consult. Our plans were to go to a tennis club and Dennis lived in the same town with the tennis club. We left a little early and went first to Dennis's house. While my date consulted with Dennis, I spent the time with two of Dennis's children. After we left, my date told me that Dennis had asked how serious we were. Learning that it was a casual relationship, Dennis asked for my phone number. My date agreed to ask my permission.

When Dennis called, I was surprised and a bit uneasy. After all, having met two of his three children, I assumed a wife/mother. He explained that he was divorced and had full custody of his three children. In all honesty, I could not even recall what he looked like.

Grooming, Gaslighting, Ranking and Comparing

On our first date, we went to the Vivian Beaumont Theater at Lincoln Center, saw Trelawney of the Wells and had a wonderful evening. Enthralled with his charming, delicious smile, intelligence, sense of ethics and wide interests, I wanted more. We had read many of the same books and enjoyed some of the same music and we both valued family. I admired that he had fought for custody of his children ages 14, 10, and almost 7 at that time. While we had vastly different religious and cultural backgrounds, there seemed to be a quality and ease to our communication.

He drove me home to my apartment on Staten Island and we talked for a long time not wanting the evening to end. I suggested we plan to see each other soon again. He looked pleased at first and then disconcerted. "Let's plan for tomorrow. In fact, let's plan lots of tomorrows! Finally, we agreed to meet at his house the following Friday and have dinner with his children. During the week, I thought about him constantly. Friday couldn't come soon enough.

DT:Manafort is wonderful, Michael Cohen has been a tremendous help, Reince Priebus, Anthony Scaramucci, and on and on..so many forced out and quit; then stated so often things like "Obama left a mess", "Hillary caused it", "that was the worst agreement NAFTA, UN, Paris Accord, etc., past administrations failed at…etc." that was and is gaslighting and grooming his followers. NAFTA is the worst agreement, the UN is totally irrelevant, China is the worst cheater, etc.

Not My Fault Syndrome

Arriving at his house, I felt a bit intimidated. On my last visit, I had scarcely noticed it, an imposing brick colonial on property that was oversized relative to others in town. A silent, dour- looking middle aged woman answered the doorbell. She opened the door and then disappeared. No greeting! There were some cooking sounds and smells from the kitchen, but no voices. After about 20 minutes Dennis arrived home from work and seemed surprised to see me there saying "Oh, you're early. Are you hungry?" I was also surprised because I was a little late as his directions were not correct. But it seemed very unimportant and I let it go.

DT: Blamed everyone, especially Obama & Hillary and the fake news for HIS failures; past administrations made "the worst agreements in history" (NAFTA, inability to reach denuclearization in North Korea, Jeff Sessions, James Comey responsible for Mueller investigation; blamed the Democrats for distorting the statistics regarding the deaths of people in Puerto Rico when it was his own administration who did the research and reporting.

Grooming, Proxy Recruitment, Goal Post Changed from Moment to Moment, Victimization

When I asked if he had had a good day, he simply responded that it had been okay. He went upstairs, changed into more comfortable clothes, came back down and checked his mail. I inquired about the children. He answered that they had eaten already. My reaction was mixed; disappointment and relief. I was happy to have some time with him alone but disappointed to not to have time with the children. We had supper and he talked a bit about his day. He was so handsome, so intelligent, a man ahead of his time, it was impossible for me not to fall in love with him. I wanted to be with him every minute. That evening we decided to get married. His proposal: I think we should get married. How about it? And we planned to do so in about 7 weeks! I was fully aware that he had three growing children and that this would be a challenge. I was ready for it with him…BUT, **with** him, not only **for** him.

DT: states that: "Manafort is a wonderful man. He has done so much! I rely on him for so much." MANAFORT WAS FIRED AFTER about FORTY-NINE DAYS AND then DISPOSED OF; then Manafort was convicted of eight felonies. Record number of WH staff fired after very short times. Michael Cohen disposed of after about 15 years of service, several (about 61%) of members of senior staff were fired on twitter,even television as with Comey, after serving for varying short amounts of time.

Yes, we were engaged on our second date and planned for a wedding in about seven weeks. Yes, I was aware that I could be impulsive and a risk taker. Yes, every member of my family and every dear friend, even colleagues exhorted me to wait longer before marrying. My dear, sometimes overprotective sister, Loretta, gently and lovingly gave me several reasons to postpone the wedding.

"Marie, you and the children need to get to know each other"," "taking on three children is more than you can believe", "what about your career"? etc., she questioned.

Self-aggrandizement, Anger

But he was a very good man and deliberately so. The younger of two sons of eastern European immigrant parents, he was born in Brooklyn and raised with his brother in Queens, New York. He wanted to teach, but his parents discouraged this in favor of a more lucrative career. Intelligent and hard-working, Dennis had achieved a master's Degree in electrical engineering from City College. More than once he stated that his preference would have been a degree in education, aiming at graduate level. He never enjoyed engineering. Yet, he consistently worked very hard at providing for his family, maintaining his family's home and achieving a better lifestyle for them than he felt he had had. He spoke begrudgingly a number of times about how resentful he was that he was not allowed to pursue a degree in education as he was convinced that he would have been a spectacular educator. It was, in fact, a recurring theme with him over the years. I would have been a spectacular professor, a teacher to make history, a winner, he would say often. When I suggested he take courses to become qualified, he RAGED! You think it is that easy? No resolution.

DT: *"I will build the most beautiful wall", "Mexico will pay for the wall." "The economy is better than it has been in xx years." There is no more worry about North Korea and nuclear war." NATO is no longer relevant. I will build a new structure. I will construct a new Health Care plan to replace Obamacare for this time in history",* etc.

Narcissism, Lying, Triangulation

As we began plans for the wedding, I was firm that it be in the Catholic Church. That was very important to me. When I approached the priest in the local parish, the requirements for that seemed excessive. Dennis's first marriage had occurred within the church and the church did not recognize divorce. So, technically, he was Catholic and divorced so, the church considered him still married. He had shared that he was an atheist but, without his father's knowledge, his mother had slipped him off to church one day with his brother and had them baptized. He also told me that the children's birth mother had had delusions which included believing that she was St. Theresa, and they felt fear regarding all things religious. We soon made plans to be married in his living room by the leader of the Humanist society next door.

The leader of the Society and Dennis made the plans for the wedding. I was sad and hurt but rationalized that it was the marriage that was important, not so much the wedding. A few years later I learned that the plans were made before I acknowledged that a Catholic marriage could not occur.

DT: The WH consistently declined to comply with subpoenas, violating the law, he has been obsessed with denigrating Obama Super critical of

Obamacare, but has not produced a replacement; denigrated the media severely, but, stopped press conferences and alienated reporters and undermined the credibility of the press, mocked and threatened them, refused to condemn Saudi Arabia for killing of Kashoggi, mocked a disabled reporter, etc.   I will release my tax returns after…… over 8 thousand documented lies in about 2 ½ years, we did a fantastic job in Puerto Rico, those people are very grateful, only about 40 people died (almost 3,000), etc. alienating so many of our allies e.g., Canada, UK, Germany, South Korea, China, etc.

The small intimate wedding was warm and personal, with only immediate family and we went to a lovely intimate restaurant nearby for a celebration lunch. Immediately after the wedding, Dennis's middle child gave me a huge hug and said, "It will be easy to call you Mom". I was fully hooked. Immediately after the ceremony, I looked for him to celebrate, but, he had gone into the library to pay bills!

We drove home where he said a very definite goodbye to the guests at the curb and thank you to everyone making it clear that the event was over, and we would see them at the reception a month later. At the curb, he asked if anyone had left anything in the house and offered to get it for them. We had agreed to have an open house reception on the two days following Christmas. He stated that we could see everyone then.

The next part of the plan was the honeymoon. He had asked me where I would like to go and, recognizing that we had only five days as he was still paying off his expensive divorce, I suggested we go to the Adirondacks, a place I loved. He agreed.

Belittling, Demeaning, Parental Alienation, Imposed Isolation

Dennis' mother babysat while we were away. As we left the house on Monday morning, I noted his baggage. Slightly over three years out of the convent, I was too naïve to realize that bringing nine books on a five-day honeymoon was remarkable and noteworthy. ⚑ A short time after driving north on the New York Thruway, we exited at a tourist spot, Howe Caverns. I assumed that the stop was for lunch but, he said he wasn't hungry ⚑ and had long wanted to see the Caverns. We drove to the Adirondacks on Thursday afternoon and left for home on Friday morning. I had lived in Lake Placid in the Adirondacks for two years, had friends there and had hoped for more time. During the five days, the only time we spent together was breakfast, dinner and bedtime. He read, napped, went alone for walks. When I asked what he was reading, the only answer was, "nothing most people would be interested in". I felt incredibly lonely and disappointed but continually made excuses "he has had so little time to himself", "I wonder if he is quietly shy," "I know how precious quiet reading time is". When we arrived home, Dennis drove his mother back to her home in Queens and I unpacked and tried to find my way around the kitchen to begin making supper…for 5!!! Dennis had told the nanny that her services were no longer needed but I didn't know that until we were home. After supper, clean up and some time with the two younger children, I went upstairs to get ready for bed but found Dennis with Eddy lying on our bed watching TV. 🚩 I definitely felt like the intruder, but said, "Oh sorry, I want to get ready for bed now". Dennis answered that there was another TV which I could use in the basement family room!

DT: Often implemented policies without informing staff; failed to appoint many cabinet members for months, had his immediate family members as staff, failed to consult with, or even inform his top national security personnel team before pulling security clearances, had failed to verify security clearances for many of the White House staff. Fake news, Crooked Hillary, Lying Ted, Mr. Magoo. Self-Imposed Isolation

<u>BE</u>GINNINGS

Narcissism, Proxy Recruitment

On our return, I focused on getting to know the children, the house, the children's schoolwork, the town, etc. and I saw Christmas as a wonderful time to begin to solidify us as a family. I wanted it to be the best Christmas the children had had in a long time. Dennis declined to state what would make it a happy day for him. So, I did my best. When I asked if he knew of things the children would like as gifts, he answered "No, you see them more than I do."

DT: Stopped having press conferences, put Sean Spicer, Sandra Sanders in his place, fired people by Twitter, Spent inordinate amounts of golf time. Rarely consulted with or made appropriate use of the top advisers in the administration.

On the morning of Christmas, I was so excited I woke up very early and waited to hear them coming downstairs. There were gifts for them that I knew they would be excited about and I could wait no longer and went downstairs to light the tree and start the special breakfast I had planned.

As soon as I plugged in the tree lights, I realized that most of the gifts were missing. Running upstairs, I woke Dennis saying "The gifts are gone. They must have been stolen. Who would do that?" "Oh, no", Dennis said, "the kids each come down when they wake up, get their gifts and open them in their rooms." Stunned, my only response was "Why?" My experience had been that this was one of the primary and major ways of learning the joy of giving. In addition, it was a family activity and tradition remembered by most for the rest of their lives.

Dt: Very soon he stopped having press conferences at all, held meetings with heads of state alone and refused to share notes, translations, etc.; Alienated so many allies, e.g., Lying Ted, Little Rocket Man, Elmer Fudd, etc., etc. NATO is obsolete, TTP is useless, Obama left a mess

Belittling, Condescending, Patronizing Parental Alienation, Triangulation

I knew the day was to be spent having Christmas dinner at his mother's home and, after breakfast asked," What time are we leaving for your mother's?" He looked surprised but happy and said "Oh, are you coming, too?" Disbelief, confusion, hurt left me speechless!

DT: Melania is rarely seen, rarely accompanies DT, rejects his touch, etc.

He fires people by tweet or even on television (James Comey), not in person.

Belittling, False Accusations, Victimization

During the pre-Christmas time, I asked about a budget and we settled on one. As he was paying bills one evening, he called me into the library asking who the two winter nightgowns were for and I said, "Oh, yes, there was a great two-for-one sale and I needed them". "Thought you could sneak them in with the holiday stuff, did you?", he sneered. "Next time, ask." I felt humiliated, hurt and confused saying, "do you want me to ask every time I need something?"

"Of course, how else can I plan finances?" You have no experience planning finances for a family. What would you know?

DT: All the false accusations about Hillary. All his belittling remarks about athletes, administrative staff, heads of state, Hillary should be locked up, why didn't Obama do something if he knew about the Russian meddling (Obama did give DT: notice in writing), Papadopoulos was a coffee boy, etc. Comey is a liar, the Democrats are sabotaging me, the fake news constantly lies, Jeff Sessions was disloyal when he recused himself, etc.

Normalization, Abusive Cycle

The following Christmas we were again on our way to his mother's house and Brian, who had given his little sister a disposable camera for Christmas was showing her how to use it. She was enthralled with it and I was happy to see them joining the fun of giving. During the afternoon at grandma's, the camera fell on the kitchen floor and broke. Anne Marie was very upset, cried and begged her brother and her father to try to fix it. They were unable to do so.

On the way home in the car and Ann Marie was still upset. Her brother suggested that she bring it back to the store and tell them that it was broken when she opened it. I began to suggest that that was not a good way to handle it and it was lying. Dennis intervened and was very clear that he thought that would be a really good way to handle it. I was dumbfounded.

Although he did seem to be guided by a moral sense, he seemed blinded when it came to guiding his children. This worried me a great deal.

Later that evening, I challenged Dennis about the ethics of his lesson.

I had not yet learned that that was neither acceptable nor effective. For more than a week there was ranting and raging and accusations every single evening. "What! Are you perfect?" "Oh, I'm sure you never told a lie.", etc. 🚩 ...rages for several days!!

Abusive   Cycle,   Silent Treatment

The first time that we were alone after that was Sunday evening after dinner so, after cleaning up, I went into the living room where he had poured himself a glass of wine. I reached for the glass intending to ask him to wait until we talked. He pulled my arm back, knocked me to the floor and walked into the library. 🚩 🚩 Too stunned to respond I went upstairs to bed thinking "Had this fool rushed in where wiser angels would have feared to tread"? I found it impossible to explain or rationalize what had happened. When he came up, I expected him to be embarrassed, contrite, apologetic…Instead, he said, "I guess you know not to take my wine from me now. I'm very touchy about that," and smiled. That began my long dilemma.

Yes, it began my VERY long dilemma. Was he just seeking an inexpensive nanny? Was he able to have an intimate relationship? What did my commitment to him mean? It was also a commitment to three children who had lost a mother to mental illness and divorce, two grandmothers, who were not able to continue caring for them, and three or four nannies within a few years. That was a lot of loss for young children, a lot!

Throughout the next years, there were six additional instances of assault for which I had him arrested four times. I still know that that was the right thing to do but it never resulted in anything other than anger additional abuse and week-long periods of silence. I never did press charges and maybe that was an error. But there was nothing in me that wanted to hurt him.

Each time he was arrested, he would call his middle child, have him bail him out of jail. Usually he would then stay with him for a few days and I would relent. I knew that had to stop but was unable to punish him that badly knowing how badly he was hurting to begin with.

There is no question that I would do that differently now. But the pain and hurt that was caused is inestimable.

Imposed Isolation, Alienation, Denigration

Our two-day open house wedding reception was pleasant. He went to the iconic Zabar's delicatessen in New York and bought huge loaves of bread, salads and cheeses. Everyone seemed to enjoy the days, or so I thought…many years later I learned that some people were appalled and hurt at things Dennis said and did. For example, in talking with a long-term friend of mine and her husband, he expressed his surprise when she answered that she had recently achieved her master's degree in Education. "Congratulations, after all, you're Polish, aren't you?", he said. And when another friend's two-year-old son climbed on our bed, Dennis admonished him, hit him on the thighs and said to them, "You'll have to show him who's boss, won't you?" That family declined to visit us ever again although I was invited to visit them many times. ⚑

It took me so long to realize that this was part of a pattern, not isolated incidents. Within a few years there was almost no one who would come to our home. My sister and brother-in-law would invite me to their home as with some friends. I would also meet friends and family at restaurants or at malls or wherever we could meet where Dennis would not be present.

I remember the Thanksgiving after Dennis's mother had passed away. My dear sister was in chemotherapy because she had developed breast cancer. I did not try to negotiate with Dennis; I simply invited my sister and her family to the house for Thanksgiving dinner. Yes, I was anxious, but I had developed a strategy that I thought might work. Dennis had a project he was anxious to complete, and I set it up to make it appealing for him to work on that for the day.

When it was time for dinner, everyone came to the dining room, found seats and began to exclaim about the good smells and their hunger.

As Dennis arrived, he walked into the dining room behind my sister's chair, reached up to the top of her head, and pulled off her scarf which she was wearing to deflect interest from her balding head. Dennis simply said, "you don't need to wear that in here. We all know you're bald."

Now it was me who felt the rage! That may be the one time I seriously did want to hurt him back. The children snickered and dived into dinner. No one else seemed very interested. Almost immediately after dinner my sister and her family politely but firmly stated that it was getting late, my sister was getting tired and they had to leave.

I never did invite them back and they gently made it clear that they preferred it that way. That was indeed an incredibly sad day and one which led to more sadness. It is also one I have still been unable to forgive a virtue which I have striven to develop and maintain all my life.

THE WOMEN IN HIS LIFE

Narcissism, Anger, False Accusations, Triangulation, Victimization

During the first several years of our marriage I had often asked about his earlier life. Rarely did he respond with more than a few words. Those words were always tinged with resentment. I knew almost nothing about his father as he had died long before I met Dennis. I knew only that his father was a tailor, an atheist and an avid reader and had been hospitalized for depression twice. He had been sent to the U.S. to make money and send it back for his family, just as my own father had done at age eleven. Dennis did not know how old his father was when he came here. I can recall no conversations about happy or unhappy times in school, with neighborhood friends, army buddies, holidays, times with his brother or parents. He did speak of feeling very isolated as a child because his parents and the two boys only spoke Lithuanian until the boys started school and they belonged to none of the more prevalent religious groups e.g. Protestant, Catholic or Jewish. The few times he spoke of his mother he used words such as, "a sneak, a liar, manipulative, a drinker, cold, and unloving". Several times he told of her leaving him home alone in his crib when she took his brother to school and/or went on errands. He remembered screaming and being frightened. If I tried to suggest that she had learned parenting at a time and in a place very different from ours, he dismissed this angrily and told me she also never put them to bed because she would sneak his father's alcohol and fall asleep early.

He also told me of a couple of times when she returned to Europe to visit her family and bring them money, she never told her sons that she was leaving. He recalled being terrified again that his mother had disappeared with no explanation and the babysitter would care for them during the day. That was one memory that he repeated often. And when he did, the Terror was still evident. But if I even hinted that those events would be frightening for a young child, he either raged that I was being critical of his mother or he abruptly and finally terminated the conversation.

The rage was obvious. But he refused to talk with her about it, stating that he needed her to babysit at times and "did not want to alienate her". I was shocked…again. Alienate her? HIS NEEDS?   Why not just communicate with her and resolve?

I also recall a few years after his brother had died, his mother was planning a trip to see her family and she called them to coordinate the plans. They told her she was too old now she should just send them money!!! Dennis thought that was wise!

DT: implementing Zero Tolerance policy for immigrants without any plan for those affected; Multiple golf trips with no regard for attention to crucial issues, or costs to taxpayers, etc. Alienation of most allies, e.g. Canada, Mexico, UK, Germany, etc., Communicating almost everyone through twitter.

Triangulation, Anger

I had gotten to know his mother well during the first few years. She and Dennis' brother, Andy, often came for Sunday dinner. They had done a lot of babysitting and were very attached to the children and the children to them. My impression of her was that she had been raised in farm country in a third world country during hard times. I never knew her to lie or drink alcohol. She sometimes told the children what she thought they wanted to hear, but in inconsequential things as parents often did at that time. While she was not physically affectionate, I found her to be very caring, to both her children and grandchildren and watched her as she did all she could to support them during Dennis's divorce and single parenthood. She could be harsh. On more than one occasion, I saw her strike the children across the face, a few times take the handle of a dinner knife and hit the elbow of one of the children who had an elbow on the table. Marcella was certainly bright, though undereducated, as were most immigrants at that time. Occasionally, she gave the children a slap on the arm. That bothered me and yet, I was afraid to approach Dennis about it. Dennis said that she always used spankings to reprimand him and his brother, too. She had more than adequate common sense, good judgement, and a good command of self-taught English. Also, she was not hesitant to make it clear that she was disappointed that her son had married "an Irish girl again." (me) The only anecdote Dennis told me about her was that she was "cheap enough to try to save money by cutting off the hems of pillowcases and sewing them onto the bottoms of the boys' pants to lengthen them."

DT: Denigration of many of his staff, world leaders, various ethnic groups as well as religious sects, colleagues, fellow members of his staff, intelligence organizations, etc. Jeff sessions, his attorney general, appointed by him was described as a dumb southerner, looking like Mr. Magoo, speaking of lying Ted, accusing Ted Cruz of being involved in the murder of JFK's, etc.

Suggestions for ICE agents to shoot immigrants in the legs to slow them down.

Lying, Imposed Isolation

Next door lived a couple just a bit older than us. It was clear that there was some strain between Dennis and them. In time, I asked him about this, and he told me they had planted a lilac bush on property that belonged to him. He had asked them to move it and they had declined. He ranted about it for some time and ended with, "Don't ask me about it again. They're irrational. And she's a drunk." That was more than 40 years ago, I am still friends with her and have never known her to drink any alcohol at all.

I did recently ask her what had caused the rift between her and Dennis. Her response was that she was not clear about it. She and her husband had invited him to play bridge early after Dennis had moved in. After a short time, she had gone to get some refreshments and when she returned, Dennis had left, and her husband simply stated that she was never to invite him back.

DT: over eight thousand documented lies in two years; alienating so many allies : Canada, UK, Germany, Mexico, etc., as well as NATO members), etc. derogatory name-calling, categorizing people by race, ethnicity, religion, gender etc.

Projection, Anger, False Accusations

It took me several years (too many) to assimilate all of this and realize that just about every significant woman in his life was **a** source of anger and disdain. In every conversation we had on the topic, his anger was evident and yet, of the instances I was familiar with, I saw no objective evidence to support his perceptions.

<u>Had it only occurred to me at the time that I WAS THE WOMAN HE LIVED WITH!!! And his perception of me was colored by his disorder in the same way. The price I and all four of his children would pay for that failure!!!</u>

DT: Rages and rants several times daily but; has instilled fear in staff and forced them into a kind of paranoia and fear of disagreeing with or crossing him, that is, LOYALTY in his eyes., he issues executive orders without consulting advisors, cabinet members, experts, the New York Times accusatory Op Ed,

OTHERS IN HIS LIFE

Abusive Cycle, Scapegoating, Not My Fault Syndrome, Proxy Recruitment

His brother, Andy, was in his late 40s, a bachelor and a graphic artist who lived with his mother. Andy seemed to be a nice person but a loner. He had never had a girlfriend that Vic knew of, had no friends, no apparent interests other than his oil painting and he clearly suffered from some level of depression which he apparently had battled for years. At one Sunday dinner, as I was clearing the table, I heard him say, "Oh, all those homosexuals are so sick. They should all be hung." Not only was that such an offensive thing to say, but, a horrible thing to have his children hear and observe. I was so repulsed that I just stayed in the kitchen until I calmed down.

I was never able to really develop a relationship with Andy. He seemed to be somewhat close to Eddy and Brian. Andy did enjoy painting and had a rather large collection of paintings he had done in his basement. But none of them were displayed anywhere else in the house. The few paintings I saw projected a significant depression. They were all seascapes and landscapes but all the subjects in the paintings were dead. Dead trees; dead shrubbery, driftwood, etc. There were none with any human subjects or anything else alive. Andy made no effort to get to know me. He in fact, avoided every opportunity. When at our house, he spent all his time with the boys.

Over time it became clear that there was a fierce loyalty among Dennis and his children, and I admired that. Yet, I also realized that there was also very little affection. Even at times of celebration, there were no hugs, no sentimental gifts, no indications of emotional connection, nor interest in spending time together or supporting the others' interests. Except for his younger son, Dennis, nor his other two children, never expressed anything I could categorize as affection. Loyalty, yes. Affection, no.

🚩 🚩 🚩

The first spring I was delighted to find that Dennis had cultivated a lovely area for a vegetable garden. I had always found gardening appealing but never had the opportunity to pursue it. An even better surprise was to find that Dennis was very knowledgeable and committed to organic gardening. For me, that was a relatively new concept. But Dennis had researched and learned a lot about it. One Saturday morning he left the house and came back with a rototiller. When I heard that he had turned off the rototiller, I went out and helped him clean and fold the black mesh covering. The smell of the freshly turned garden was so good and I remarked on it. Dennis looked surprised and said, "it's just dirt, Marie." I heard that as lightly teasing. And just asked him where we would start. "In the dirt, Marie." "I know Vic, but what can we do first? Is there anything more to do to prepare for the seeds?" "No, I'll get some seeds next weekend." 🚩 I was getting excited and asked him if he had any books so I could learn more about organic gardening. He promised to leave two of them out on the desk in the library. When he left to return the rototiller, I went and got two of the books and began reading. There was a lot to learn and I was eager to do so.

The following weekend he went to the local country store and bought so many plants; many tomatoes, lettuce, string beans, peas and we brought them out to the garden. By midmorning we had all the plants in, and I was excited. He had gleaned so many good ideas too. For example, when he cut the grass, he used the clippings between the rows of plants and explained the many benefits of that. It prevented water from evaporating and weeds from growing. He also kept a small bucket outside for kitchen refuse. As that decayed, it became fertilizer for the garden. We spent several Saturdays getting the garden underway. I enjoyed every minute of it. The gardening was fun but for us to spend time together was even more important to me. Once the garden was fully planted, he stopped attending to it at all leaving it entirely to me. I didn't mind because for me it was a pleasure. But I was hoping it would be something we would do together.

DT: Had his "fixer", used Sarah Sanders, abused during press events, but will not do them himself, used Kelley Anne Conway to take the blame for his lies, distortions, etc., sends Pence to do the difficult presentations, etc. Always BLAMED someone else for any lack of perfection in himself.

Targeted Humor, Proxy Recruitment

Through the following years, he would do the very heavy work, e.g., the tilling, lifting heavy bags of fertilizer, etc. but then he would leave. The garden became mine to attend. I thoroughly enjoyed it despite the disappointment that he withdrew. And with his guidance for first year, it was very successful. Our property was next door to the Humanist society where there was a playground. After the Sunday meetings, many people went out to the backyard with their children and they could see our garden from there. Some came over to look more closely and each time that happened, Dennis would find a reason to say, "it's even better, because I have free labor" and point to me. It was cute, not offensive, and true. However, in the years to come I look back on it and see it differently. I realized that it was part of his MO.

DT: Sending M. Pompeo and ten R. Giuliani to negotiate in Ukraine, a treacherous position. Using Michael Cohen as his "fixer"; and then disposing of him.

Belittling, Condescending and Patronizing .

Often, after the BECS platform meeting on Sunday mornings and then lunch, we went to a local park. The children played, and we had time to talk. There was so much I wanted to share with him and learn about him, I looked forward to any time we had together. One of the things I wanted to tell him too was that after working at Willowbrook Developmental (WDC), an institution for the developmentally disabled, for about two years before we were married, I had received a significant promotion and concomitant raise which had not yet come through. I felt he would like to know as it might help a bit with his divorce debt, and it had a rather unique tale attached to it. The institution had been sued for neglect and abuse by the families of the residents and had won. The resulting court order regulated most aspects of resident life but also ordered that the population be reduced from just over six thousand to about four hundred within four years. To implement this, a deputy director was appointed for each borough of the city. Each deputy had to develop a team to identify the residents from their borough, and to plan for services for them within their own borough. The Deputy Director for Brooklyn held a meeting to explain to one group of employees what that implied for them. On the way to the meeting, I saw a newspaper on the ground, picked it up but did not find a garbage can. A few days after the meeting, I was summoned to meet with the same Deputy Director who was forming his steering committee and wanted me to be his administrative assistant. Clarifying the job description, I accepted. Months later, I asked why and how he had chosen me from that large group. "Because you were reading the Wall Street Journal.", he said. (To this day, I have never read it, but cleaning litter got me a $15K raise in 1973!)

I thought Dennis would enjoy the story. Instead, he responded "Oh, so you never really **earned** the promotion." He grinned and gave me a hug. Why then did I feel so deflated, so let down?

Some months later, the check did arrive, I deposited it, and told Dennis that the check was in the checking account. Very shortly, the money had been spent and I assumed that it had been used to reduce his legal bills from his divorce. When I mentioned that, more rages! "What are you doing now checking on my money management?", "You have no idea of how to manage money for a family."," Why are you snooping into the checkbook?"

DT: Barrage of Obama criticisms, Obama was a failure, weak, he even spied on me during the campaign; it was all Obama's fault; projection of false criticisms of Obamacare, etc. Crooked Hillary, Jeff Sessions should investigate who wrote that op Ed about me, etc.

Scapegoating, Disassociation, Gaslighting, Anger, Triangulation, Denial

One weekend about a year or so after we were married, I got a call from the parents of a classmate of his older son, Eddy. They sounded distressed stating that boys had been there during the afternoon and had tried using LSD. They described Dennis's son as uncontrollable and needed us to come immediately. We arrived within a few minutes and found both boys irrational, and incoherent. Dennis immediately tried to bring his son outside but by the time we were on the lawn his son was combative. Dennis removed his belt, put it around his son's legs and we carried him three blocks home. Dennis said, "I'll take care of this" and dismissed me. I respected that he wanted to deal with this issue between himself and his son. Frankly, I was relieved as well. I never knew what passed between them. Dennis never came to bed that night and there was no conversation about the event. Weeks later I heard him talking to someone at BECS about the event telling them that Eddy was "pushing the limits" and had had "a few beers" with a friend. There was a knowing glance between the two fathers and the conversation ended. I accepted that Dennis had no reason or obligation to tell anyone what had actually happened. But that evening I gently approached the topic asking Dennis if he was worried about the experimentation with LSD. Immediately he went into a rage, screamed at me that there was no LSD, accused me of lying about it and "probably telling half neighborhood.

What are you, crazy?", and took a book off the shelf hitting me on the side of my head knocking me off my feet. As he left the room, he pushed me out of his way with his foot. I left the house and went to my sister's home. For months, I was not able to make any sense of the event, nor was I able to come to peace with it or rationalize it or accept blame for it, etc. Yet, the ever-present FEAR paralyzed me. I understood not wanting to see my child as a drug abuser risk. And, I understood that denial is a defense mechanism available to us to prevent our egos from being overloaded. But that was not the issue. Dennis simply denied the fact that his son had tried LSD although I was now certain that this was a fact. No amount of rationalizing left me peaceful. It did not keep me awake at night and was not present in my thought's day by day. But when the memory did arise there was always a sense of dis-ease. I also was concerned that a matter as important as that might not have been addressed.

DT: campaign and presidency – "fake news, alternate facts, inauguration crowd size, etc.; "It is all a hoax", Rigged Investigation; Fake news, etc. Disordered perception to the extent that reality was obliterated, i.e. disassociation

Normalization, Victimization, Self-Aggrandizement

It was only weeks later when I walked through the living room toward the library and realized that Dennis and Eddy were each lying on one of the loveseats talking. My first reaction was to be pleased that they were having some together time. It took me about fifteen to twenty minutes to accomplish the tasks I had gone into the library to do. I was not inclined to eavesdrop but could hear the conversation. My reaction was that the two were carrying on what I then began to term a "dual monologue".

Dennis would say "They're not appreciating me at work. I could be so much more productive."

His son responded, "I wish I had a better math teacher. The guy I have, never explains anything. He just tells you what you should learn and assigns homework."

His father would respond, "I could turn some of those committees into a team of whiz kids. I can't stand watching some of those jerks plodding along and getting nothing done."

The next response from his son would be, "that high school should get rid of the dumb teachers and get some good ones."

Followed by, "It's such a bureaucracy at work that no one wants to tackle it. Soon I'll be positioned to do it. They'll see." And on it went.

DT: – "Make America Great Again, I will create more jobs than anyone else can. I will get rid of ISIS in days, will drain the swamp, Mexico will pay for the wall, etc. the economy is better than it has been in 100 years. I have done that. (Untrue) I will hire the best people (many of them have now been indicted for major crimes). "Drain the Swamp" !!!

Normalization, Gaslighting, Victimization, Projection

I still can't name my reaction to that; surprise, confusion, baffled? But I do know that in some ways it later helped clarify something. In the meantime, I frequently returned to it and wondered, "am I expecting too much, in terms of communication? Is this part of the cultural difference, i.e. my Irish family had a few times been described as "over communicators"; that would impact my expectations.

Was the Eastern European style of communicating that different? Would it help to adjust my expectations? That conversation seemed to satisfy them. Could I adjust to that? It never occurred to me that I did not seem to have problems communicating with others. But it did occur to me that I could never be satisfied with that kind communication. A new dilemma: I was certainly willing to try to accommodate to some extent, but I could not accept that what I had observed was communication.

DT: Gaslighting, The Mueller Investigation is rigged, a witch hunt, and a hoax, the Democrats are lying about me and sabotaging my success.

Another incident occurred a few months later. I went to Eddy's room to tell him something. I saw a tank with two iguanas in it. He had stopped on the way home from school to buy some white mice to feed the iguanas.

That was not something I wanted to witness. But what was striking, was the big smile on Eddy's face. He did not usually smile easily but it was obvious that he was enjoying this. *When I said,* "You actually enjoy that, Eddy?" He responded," Sure do, it's fun." It left me cold. Again, I made excuses" I never had brothers, I've always disliked reptiles, I guess boys are just different."

Parental Alienation, False Accusations, Victimization

When Eddie was graduating from high school, he had apparently arranged with his father to have a big graduation party at the society next door. I knew nothing of it. In fact, I had asked Dennis if he wanted to have a family party for his son's graduation. He declined.

One evening a few days before or after the graduation, I don't remember, Eddy went out and said he wouldn't be back until late. A few hours later his father came home and was obviously in a rage. He stated that Eddie had called him at work and told him that the party had been called off by the society because the agreement was that there would be no alcohol. I did not even know that the party was happening. Dennis went over to the society and I could hear the I rants and screaming from the house. When I went over to the building, most of the students who were at the party were leaving for having friends pick them up. Obviously, the party was ending.

There was chaos and confusion which I had become accustomed to and there was little I could do, so I just returned to the house. A good bit later Dennis came home in a rage. He ranted for hours about how irresponsible I was to allow alcohol at a party of minors. I understood that he was upset and embarrassed in front of his peers at the society. I understood that he was upset with his son for the whole event. But, as far as I know, did not address any of the issues with Eddie but simply scapegoated me. I understand that I had no responsibility for any of the events. I did not, and I could not.

There was little point to trying to resolve any of the issues that needed to be addressed that night. But I did leave the house; did not sleep in the hammock in the back yard as I had done in the past, but this time went to friend's home and spent the night there to avoid the raging and ranting.

The anger lasted for weeks and there was no rational attempt to resolve any of it.

DT: trump raged for months about the special investigator, what he called Comey's betrayal, Jeff session's failure to notify him of his intention to recuse himself, etc. but never made any attempt to resolve the issues or improve the protocols that led to any of them.

Victimization, Anger, Narcissism, Scapegoating

I did not meet Dennis's first wife until about two years after we were married when she came to visit her children. The relationship between her and the children was tenuous and strained. She had been hospitalized for extended periods after the birth of each child. I never knew if the reason was her paranoid schizophrenia or postpartum depression or both. Dennis only stated that she was "crazy"," a liar", "an *addict*", a "thief" and "manipulative". I tried to point out that her delusions were real to her and while, maybe untrue, were not really lies either; or her addiction was to prescriptions for her serious illness. He never expressed sadness for her or his children who suffered because of her illness...only disdain, self- pity, victimization and anger, anger, anger… 🚩

DT: *the investigation led by Mueller, appointed by him, and 13 democrats (not true) are obstructing my administration's progress, favoritism and scapegoating*

.

Demeaning, *Parental Alienation, Normalization, Triangulation, Invalidation, Gaslighting,* **Victimization, Anger**

A few months before Ann Marie turned 18 her father got a call saying that the children's birth mother had passed away. They were, of course a bit upset but had not seen her in quite some time. The following day I received a call telling us of the arrangements for the funeral. They all arranged to have the day off. On that morning I came downstairs with my daughter prepared to accompany them. Dennis said, "Where are you going?" "With you, of course." "Why would you go? You never even knew her." I was immobilized. But it also (finally!) made it 100% clear that he had no sense of me as their stepmother.

DT: Objectification, Invalidation, Alienation, Gaslighting, Narcissism, Victimization

Why did I not leave them then? Why did that not have enough meaning for me to realize that my role was strictly limited to nanny/housekeeper? I have multiple answers for that; I had made a commitment to four people; the children had had a tumultuous early childhood, we had a relatively challenging marriage, etc. But none were or are adequate.

According to Dennis's first divorce decree the house belonged to him until the youngest child was 18 years old. At that time, the house was to be sold and the proceeds divided equally; or one or the other could party could buy the other out. A few months later I said to Dennis, "you were very lucky with the timing of Mary Ann's death. Now you own the house free and clear." "Yeah, that bitch wouldn't even give me a decent fight at the end."

DT: Obama left a mess, why did he do nothing about the meddling by the Russians, etc. (untrue), Obama's economy depleted our economic resources (untrue).

Gaslighting, lying, Narcissism, Triangulation, Proxy Recruitment

In fact, the house now belonged to Dennis and the estate of his first wife (Eddy, as executor). I waited for a couple of years hoping Dennis would suggest putting the house in both our names. He never did. Eventually, I went to him and asked if he had the intention to do that. "Why would I?" he asked. "Because we have been married quite a long time, I have cared for the house during those years, because it's the decent thing to do." No response.

 "He is not mean, he is not bad; his disordered world is all he has.; he is doing his best; his best, is not something I can detest".

DT: *using Kellyanne Conway, Sean Spicer, Sandra Sanders, even Michael Kelley etc. Pence as spokespeople having gaslighting them as proxies, triangulation but with the entire country and his own administrative staff. Demeaning*

THE WEDDINGS

Demeaning, False Accusations

Eddy had graduated from college. There was a huge number of students graduating at a large stadium. I always sought an opportunity for humor and remember one funny incident. One Asian young man was receiving his doctoral degree and, when they announced him, he was presented as, "Dr. Ding Dong". I envisioned that young man going through life with that name. When I noted that to Dennis, he accused me of racism, discrimination and cruelty.

🚩

*DT: Mexicans come into our country and are rapists, drug dealers, Africans should go back to their s**t hole countries, Democrats don't know anything, all the demeaning names he* *called, both his appointees and persons such as Kim Jon UN, many others.*

Alienation, Normalizing, Demeaning

His oldest son's graduation went well and soon after that Dennis's son announced that he was engaged. We had met his fiancée a few times and I really liked her. As tradition played out, most of the wedding plans were made by the bride's family and her. They were extremely gracious about informing/consulting us about the plans and asking for and accepting our input. All of Dennis's children were to be in the wedding party.

Dennis was unrelenting in criticizing her, e.g., she just sees Eddy as a check book, she has no professional goals, she is only interested in having babies and a funding source, etc.

A couple of weeks before the wedding, Eddy did some travel for work. When he returned, he came to our house for supper one night. After supper, I heard him talking to his brother about a brief affair he had had while away. I was disgusted, but not surprised. In talking with his brother, he had said that the woman's name was Beverly. They talked a bit more and he left for home. About a year or more later, after the wedding, they told us that we were to become grandparents. We invited them for dinner to celebrate and invited his brother and sister of course.

During the time between the invitation and the dinner they had bought a new car. When all gathered, there were congratulations, catching up and general chatter. Dennis' Brian asked if they had come in the new car and said he wanted to see it. His older brother responded, "Oh no, we just put a saddle on her," nodding toward his very pregnant wife. They all laughed. His new wife was not a small person, was very pregnant and had been retaining fluids during the pregnancy. I was pained for her. The conversation went on after dinner and came to questions about baby names. The soon to be father said that if it was a girl, he was hoping to name her "Beverly". Knowing grins past among the three men. I left the room and went upstairs furious, angry and disdainful.

The wedding had been planned with great detail and caring. During the weeks, just prior to the wedding it became clear that the groom was having second thoughts. He used no discretion and no filter and no sensitivity when making this clear. Everyone in the two immediate families was upset, sad and worried. Only a couple of days before the wedding did he concede by saying, "okay, let's just get it done." When the day came Dennis came downstairs in his tuxedo. I had never seen him in a tux, and he looked ever so handsome. I told him that and he was clearly pleased. I guess I was hoping that he would return the compliment. Nothing.

The wedding occurred and was lovely except that it felt quite joyless. The ceremony, venue, the food, and music were all delightful. The missing piece was joy. At times when I look at the pictures, almost everyone in both immediate families looked years older than they were and smiles are rare and stilted.

Brian's wedding was over all delightful. Clearly, they had worked together with both families, and then brought them together for a lovely day of celebration.

Shortly after that, we received a call from Ann Marie that she was becoming engaged. We had not met her intended husband and invited them for dinner, so we could get to know each other. In recollection, it made no sense, but I planned a dinner to please Dennis, not the new couple. Fear, not joy, guided my decision. Although I certainly wanted to please the newly engaged couple, I was more fearful of provoking Dennis.

Demeaning, Anger, Rages, Scapegoating

Introductions were made, and some small talk occurred and was pleasant.

Ann Marie was very gracious and made the conversation simple, pleasant, and inclusive. Relieved, I went to the kitchen to complete preparations for dinner. When ready, I went and invited everyone to the dining room. Dennis stayed in the living room. He was in his recliner, reading the newspaper. I gave him a few minutes and then went in to nudge him. His reply was, "I'm not having dinner with that buffoon." I was stupefied, almost paralyzed, momentarily unable to react. It took about 10 minutes to coax him to do it for Ann Marie. He did finally come to the dining room but, remained almost silent throughout most of dinner. Try as I may I was unable to prompt him to conversation. After the couple left, he ranted and raged about how "dumb, childish, unambitious, inadequate" his son-in-law to be was. He disparaged and demeaned him for about two hours. The rant continued for weeks. And soon it grew to rages about both of his children marrying "idiots, both have no brains, no ambition and only want a checkbook. One is only a hairdresser and the other a mommy". I had some understanding of feeling that no one was good enough for your child. However, this was so extreme, it concerned me greatly. I had learned by now that trying to reason with him would only lead to more raging and ranting and he would see it as disagreeing with him or criticizing him. That was not permitted.

"He is not mean; he is not bad; his disordered world is all he has.; he is doing his best; his best is not something I can detest."

DT: Invalidation - Lebron James, Jeff Sessions, all Democrats, etc. were dumb, inadequate, ineffective, sabotaging his own success, deceptive.

When I married her father, Ann Marie was six years old. From that time, I had been impressed with her organizational skills. She never lost gloves, never misplaced school items, never lost keys, always had what she needed for school ready and always had everything in its right place. How did she do that? The trait continued into her adulthood. For her wedding everything was planned, lists made and checked off, no details were omitted. I bought some pots of flowers that matched her bouquet, went with her to buy her wedding dress, and assisted where I could. The day before the wedding she came to our house as we had planned a brunch for the females in the wedding party. The night before she was getting somewhat anxious and decided to rent a movie to distract herself. On the way, she turned her ankle and by the time she got home it had already begun to swell. I felt so bad for her. We got ice and aspirin and elevated her foot and did everything we could. I went out early the next morning and bought her a pair of white ballet slippers in case she could not wear her shoes. It did not look good for the next day.

On the wedding day, her ankle seemed better than we had expected, and we had a lovely brunch in the backyard. The day was beautiful and because the wedding was outdoors that meant so much. She got dressed, and ready to go and appeared to be relatively calm. The time came, and we left for the wedding venue. The area was decorated beautifully, and a four-piece orchestra began to play about fifteen minutes before the wedding time. People were congregating, and all the wedding party was there except for her oldest brother. We waited and waited. Almost an hour later he arrived and finally the wedding could begin.

The ceremony was lovely and, while brief, offered an air of joy and celebration. Because the ceremony began so late, I had spoken with staff to be sure that the kitchen was aware of the delay. They were wonderful. The reception began with some hors d'oeuvres and drinks for the guests. The bridal party and their families went inside and began to enjoy the event. After pictures, the music was wonderful, the food delicious and everything was going beautifully as the dancing got underway.

After about an hour and a half, many were becoming aware that the dramatic dancing of Eddy was becoming salacious and offensive. I spoke to Dennis about it and he remarked, "Oh, your pious ex nun friends are offended, are they?" (I had invited no ex nuns to the wedding.) Very gently I said, "no, Dennis, just watch." He sneered at me, "Grow up. You always pick on him. Go back to your holy roller nuns." Three or four families of guests left; others spent time outside._

"He is not mean, he is not bad; his disordered world is all he has.; he is doing his best; his best; his best, is not something I can detest."

False Accusations, Belittling, Demeaning, Proxy Recruitment

Since the wedding had been delayed by almost an hour, the band leader for the reception came and asked if we wanted to extend their engagement by an hour. I spoke with Dennis and he said to ask Ann Marie. She was thrilled because the reception was at its peak. I went back to the band and requested an additional hour. That was when they told me that they would only accept cash for that hour. I had already confirmed with the bride and groom that the reception would be extended, and the MC had announced it. There were cheers. Now we were committed but it was in the days before ATMs existed. Between Dennis and me we had less than 25% of the cash needed. When I told him that, he sneered and said, "Well you made the deal. Figure it out." The only resource I could think of was that the couple had received many cards for the wedding and there might possibly be cash in some of them. I gave some sort of explanation to the bride and took her gifts into the lady's room, locking myself in one of the stalls. I have never felt sleazier. Happily, there was enough cash. I made a list of the cards, and gifts and stopped opening the cards as soon as I had enough cash. Returning to our table I explained to Dennis what I had done. Again, he sneered and asked, "O yeah, and how much did you pocket?"

DT: Innumerable false accusations about Hillary, Obama, Endless examples from his documented over 8,000 lies, insults, false accusations and generally demeaning remarks; insulting, belittling, demeaning nicknames for both his staff, senior government officials, foreign leaders, etc.

After the wedding, I asked Eddy why he was so late. "The shoes I picked up with the tux weren't comfortable, so I had to find ones I could dance in."!!!

A few years after Ann Marie's wedding, she informed us that they were expecting a baby. Of course, there was great joy and excitement. Her pregnancy seemed to go very well and then her husband called to say that they had a healthy baby girl. When we went to visit, Ann Marie looked tired but very happy. Their daughter was healthy and beautiful, and everyone was so pleased. Two or three days later, mother and baby were discharged in good health. During her pregnancy, I had asked Dennis if he had any concerns about Ann Marie having any difficulties with postpartum depression as a mother had had. Another rage and accusations of being "the voice of doom".

"He is not mean, he is not bad; his disordered world is all he has.; he is doing his best; his best, his best, is not something I can detest." This time his raging lasted for a few months.

About two or three days after the mother and baby had been discharged, I received a call from the new daddy. He was very concerned because Ann Marie was showing very little interest in the baby, did not want to feed her and seemed "down". I asked if he wanted me to come and he replied immediately, "yes, please if you can." When I got to their house, Ann Marie was lying in bed and the baby was in the living room with her father. When I went in to see Ann Marie, she was still in the clothes she had left the hospital in. Ann Marie was something of a clean/neat nick. She did not express any response to my arrival; did not seem happy I was there, annoyed that I had arrived or any other emotional response. I talked to her for a few minutes and could feel the depression immediately. It was a gorgeous day, so I suggested that she put on sneakers and we go for short walk. She looked a bit alarmed and said, "Oh no. What if I let go of the stroller and the baby goes into a tree and dies?" As a psychiatric social worker who had worked in both pediatric units and an NICU, I recognized these as potential signs of postpartum depression and that she wanted the baby GONE.

Now I was really alarmed! So, I agreed and suggested instead that she come into the kitchen and we would have some lunch. She was reluctant but said she would be right there. When she came into the kitchen, she sat down but was completely silent, even morose. After a few minutes she said, "you know mom, I can see inside their heads now." "Really Ann Marie, whose heads can you see inside of?" "Well, Jeffrey Dahmer and people like him." While I am a psychiatric social worker, I was fully aware that this was beyond me. I simply said, "you look very sad Ann Marie. I'd like to call your obstetrician and maybe you can see him today or tomorrow." "Yeah okay his number is right here." And she handed me her phone book. I called him right away and his office was wonderful. They immediately offered to have a psychiatrist come to the house to see Ann Marie. Within an hour, the psychiatrist and a psychologist with her arrived and were wonderful. After spending a short time alone with Ann Marie, she came out to the kitchen and told me she was going to go to the drugstore and would bring back a prescription. I asked if she wanted me to go but she declined.

Very shortly after that, she returned with the medication and spent a little more time with Ann Marie. Then she came out to me and confirmed that Ann Marie was in a serious postpartum depression and she was quite concerned. She said that she was going to ask me to sign an affidavit that Ann Marie would not be left alone with the baby until she, the doctor, approved of that.

I took a few weeks off from work and went out to their house each day while Ann Marie's husband was working. I could keep up with important issues at work when I went home in the evening. It was painful to watch her struggling just to get through the day. But within a few days she did begin to take something of an interest in the baby. She also started taking care of herself better. She offered no resistance to taking the medication and within a very short time I began to see a lifting of the depression. I felt enormously relieved and so much enjoyed her beginning to bond with her daughter. By the end of about three weeks, I could see the old Ann Marie and her husband told me the same. On one of the last days I was there, Ann Marie's husband took her to the psychiatrist, and I was released from the conditions in the affidavit.

Lack of Empathy for his daughter and me, Proxy Recruitment, Narcissism

As I should have expected, there was absolutely no interest from Dennis about the event and I didn't want him to go into a rage over the phone telling me that I was exaggerating and continued to be "the voice of doom". Not one of them ever said thank you; not Ann Marie, her husband nor Dennis.

Also, for years I had had so many people call me "Pollyanna" seeing me as one who always expected good results even when others saw the obstacles. The confusion mounted.

DT:: The zero-tolerance policy regarding immigrants and the resulting damage and came to over 3000 children, the lack of planning beforehand and action afterward as well as his unwillingness to provide any resources to repair the damages demonstrate his lack of empathy; there are endless other examples and in fact, characterize his entire approach to life and his governing. Lack of attention to the devastating impact of hurricane Maria and the lying about the number of people who died because of the lack of attention.

Perceived Criticism, Silent Treatment, Self-Aggrandizement,

Once Dennis spoke of a woman, a member of the Humanist society, he had dated for a short time, but stated that she was a "money chaser" and had lied about her job, exaggerating it so that she sounded very important. He was convinced that she was interested in him only because he had such an impressive job and owned one of the biggest houses in the neighborhood. When he decided that, he stopped dating her without confronting her or trying to determine if he was correct. When I suggested that he seemed quick, maybe even harsh to find lies, there was silence…for several days.

DT: I have done more for this economy than any other administration, the fear of nuclear development by North Korea is over, this was the greatest tax cut in history, etc.

Belittling, Condescending and Patronizing, Grandiosity, False Accusations, Anger, Not My Fault Syndrome, Self-Aggrandizement

Apparently, Dennis wanted to become more involved with the humanist society. He joined one of the committees which met monthly and took on some of the responsibilities of that committee. I asked which committee he had joined, and his response was, "you don't really know about any of them, do you?" "I do, from talking with some of the members. That's why I wondered." "Well, you'll see the results if I can get that dumb chairwoman to get out of my way. She lies about how much she knows and then can't produce. She's useless, even worse. Half the time I think she's drunk by the time she comes to the meetings." Almost every time he came back from one of the meetings, he would talk and talk about how he could do a much better job with the committee and the society if she would just "get out of his way".

He spent hours talking about what great improvements he could make for them and how his revolutionary ideas would move the goals of the committee so far forward by decades. He was almost never explicit about what those goals were but seemed extremely confident that they would greatly benefit the society. If I asked for any explanation of those goals, he simply dismissed my inquiries, demeaned me and made it clear that I was not capable of comprehending them.

DT: firing of James Comey on twitter with no explicit reason as to why, his declaration that the threat of nuclear war was over without any presentation of the agreements made, his emphatic statements that his meeting with Putin was a remarkable success but his refusal to have anyone present during that meeting or to reiterate any of the discussion or agreements made at that meeting, his recent declaration that his success after the hurricane Maria in Puerto Rico was an unsung success, etc.

Belittling, Condescending and Patronizing, Grandiosity, False Accusations, Anger, Not My Fault Syndrome, Victimization

Several years later, he decided to become president of the society. I still don't know what the process entailed, but he did become president. He became very much preoccupied with his new position and spent hours reading, preparing talks, writing papers and letters, etc. I had not seen him looking that satisfied in as long as I could remember. But, when I said that to him, he became furious. He accused me again of being the voice of doom, never satisfied and overly critical. Trying to clarify, I said "Dennis, I am happy for you. I'm glad you found an arena in which you find so much satisfaction." "You don't know what you're talking about."

Where had my long-held reputation for being a Pollyanna, come from and why had it persisted for so long?

DT: the fake news, the Mueller investigation is a hoax and rigged, Bob Woodward lied about him in his book, Manafort was a good person but the Democratic (incorrect) was rigged against him, and on and on.

It seemed that any approach to him brought us into full-scale conflict. After that, I withdrew almost completely and sought shelter in the aloneness. It also became clear that at every conflict, his immediate response was to lay blame, not find a resolution; never a compromise, never negotiating, **never an insight**…never.

DT: there are innumerable examples; he wanted his big beautiful wall built and used vulnerable children to get his way.; Most recently he is almost desperate to identify the author of the New York Times op-ed piece and apparently is prepared to break the law to get this done; he is unwilling/unable to negotiate any compromise or attend to any other major issues.

Proxy Recruitment, Bullying, Anger, Victimization

Weeks after we were engaged, I grasped that we had never discussed whether or not I should resign from my job. Both Dennis and I had just assumed that I would. Next, I realized that I feared addressing this with him now. Feared?! FEARED? This realization impacted me very painfully (finally). "What was our relationship?" I questioned, pondered, worried. BUT I did not think of addressing it with

Dennis. Why? FEAR!? His moods were so volatile, so fragile, so extreme.

A few times I had a momentary vision of him wrapped in opaque shrink-wrap unable to connect with anyone or anything outside of himself. Now I think that that was a very apt description of how he went through the world so alone, so disconnected, so defensive. While it was so sad, I could find no way to help.

DT: narcissism, bullying, anger, profection. Most of the Republican Congress people are so intimidated by him that they are failing seriously in the responsibilities of representing the American people and their explicit role of providing checks and balances.

Narcissism,   Silent   Treatment, Anger

From early on Dennis had described himself as something of a movie buff. "But I don't like just any movie, only the better ones." And I asked, "and what are some of the ones you consider "better"? "Well, I review the ones showing and I picked the best." About six or seven times he suggested we go and see a movie in the evening and I always agreed. We would look through the paper and select two or three that either or both of us had an interest in. On two occasions, I made it clear that I had a preference for one of them. We would leave and, in every case, he drove to the movie of his choice. Trying to negotiate that once led to one of his rages. He just drove home. We tried once again, and the same thing happened. I simply let him get out of the car, moved into the driver's seat, and drove to the movie I wanted to see. I did not care how he got home, how angry he was but only decided that whether he was aware of it or not I was real, had some preferences and if necessary, would take care of them myself. That led to two to three weeks of silent punishment. No discussion, no negotiating, no explanation was ever sought. Neither was there ever another movie night. Or, at least I don't think there was. He would sometimes leave the house in the evening, return two or three hours later and go to sleep in the basement.

DT: silent treatment, narcissism, self-isolation, noncommunication, unwilling and/or unable to compromise, negotiate, or formulate any resolutions relative to the problems.

Demeaning, Gaslighting, Parental Alienation

It was several years before we learned that when we left the house for a movie the boys would lock their little sister, then 7 to 8 years old, in her unlit closet, threatening her if she told. When I learned this and told

Dennis, it was just another rage and name calling event with accusations that I was again lying about Eddy.

In the afternoons, each of the children came home from school at a different time. I was pleased about that because I could spend a few minutes with each one of them alone and get to know them better. Soon it became clear that Eddy, now about 16, seemed unable to engage in an actual conversation. When I sat down with him for his snack after school, to ask him about school or what you do later. The response was very often something like, "I wish I had more time to cook. I really like cooking." I would respond, "what would you like to cook; I'll buy what you need." That would be followed by "the job at Burger King is okay, but I would rather be working with machines." If I asked which machines he would respond "any machines. I just don't like to work with the public." After 15 or 20 minutes, there seemed to be no common thread to the conversation. Soon I mentioned this to Dennis very gently asking him if he had noticed the same. As I said the words the realization came to me that my attempts at conversations with both Dennis and his son were strikingly similar. I understood well that he might feel that I was being critical of his son and very carefully avoided anything that could sound critical or offensive. He looked at me with what I would describe as his sneer. Then he said, "Marie, he's a 16-year-old boy. Why would he want to talk to you?" I hadn't yet learned that that was not really a question. So, I said, "Well, I'm his new stepmother and he might want to get to know me. "Are you nuts?", he said.

DT: Narcissism,   Alienation, Contradiction of his entire intelligence institutions   even   among   the international community, in fact, his betrayal of those institutions and denigration of them.

During the first year and a half, I had been so preoccupied getting to know the children, house, town, schools, schedules, etc. that I had not been aware of my own needs or our marriage in general. He seemed quite satisfied with the way things were. Gradually, an awareness developed that Dennis gave me no indication that he had any interest in me at all, my past, my needs or desires; he never once asked me how I was doing in terms of the adjustment to step parenthood, a different house, etc. nor did he have any interest in spending time with me. With some anxiety, I carefully broached this with him accepting most of the responsibility by recognizing that I had been very preoccupied. No answer! But I had been learning the signs; he felt criticized and anger was looming. No more discussion.

Another major factor was that I was acutely aware that my dear mother had had eleven pregnancies and only two live births; my sister had suffered several miscarriages and had adopted three children. And I was nearing thirty-six. Almost immediately after marrying Dennis, I had begun fertility testing and treatment. He agreed that he would like one or even two more children. That made me happy as he might be able to enjoy them more than he had in the past as his life was more stable now. He smiled, but said, "Yeah, and I'll have more bills!" Glub!

Narcissism, False Accusations

About a year and a half of fertility treatment and I was finally pregnant! Thrilled, a bit anxious, but so excited I called Dennis at work to tell him. His response so deflated me that I simply hung up on him. "Did you find someone with stronger sperm?" About two months later I had a miscarriage. I called Vic at work to tell him that I was at Englewood Hospital and had lost the baby. "Will you be at home on time to be there for the kids?" he asked. It was never mentioned again. 🚩

Demeaning, False Accusations, Narcissism

Because that pregnancy had progressed for a few months the doctor felt a D&C should be done. I was mildly sedated for the procedure. At some moment, I heard someone step on metal garbage can and heard it open and close. In my sedated state, I pictured the fetus being disposed of then. When I said this to Dennis, he said it was stupid, because there are guidelines for disposing of a fetus. To this day, 38 years later, I cringe when I hear the same noise. Foolishly, I mentioned this to Dennis seeking support. He accused me of "hallucinating and being just as crazy as 'her'". 🚩

DT: the ravages of the hurricanes in Puerto Rico were record-breaking; the response of DT: was almost nil. The response to the reports of the children harmed by the zero-tolerance policy provoked no action on his part. As his staff diminished largely because of the failure of his White House to vet them was almost zero.

False Accusations, Scapegoating, Narcissism

I had two more miscarriages over the next two years but only mentioned them to him not wanting to be hurt more. He never questioned how I felt or anything else, never asked anything. Sadness was the predominant feeling I had but It was compounded because of the lack of support, empathy, sharing, deep, deep aloneness. How long that lasted I don't remember but I do recall that it was replaced with the growing awareness that my husband felt no sadness although it was his child too.

The awareness brought me to wonder: did he feel anything other than the anger he displayed so often? Did he feel anything toward me? It was about the same time that I began to be aware that the relationship between Eddy and Dennis seem to be less antagonistic. Initially, that seemed to be a positive thing. But soon I had to face the possibility that he had simply exchanged the scapegoat, the target of his rages. Again, what was my meaning to him? Taking stock, the only roles I seemed to play in his life were housekeeper, nanny, and scapegoat. In fact, although I tried to deny it and vehemently defend against seeing it and certainly accepting it, there soon came a time where I had to accept that his anger and rages had been transferred from Eddy to me, and only me.

I also noted, eventually, that his raging and his rants almost always occurred when no one else was nearby. Occasionally, he would become annoyed with one of the children. But those responses were always within the norm. At the time, I was not using the word "scapegoat" and spent a couple of years trying to determine if he simply hated me or needed someone to direct his rage at. Again, the fear of provoking him lead me to let the issue go for far too long. I had already become a hypervigilant person and had gotten better at evaluating how close to the surface his rages were.

"He is not mean, he is not bad; his disordered world is all he has.; he is doing his best, his best, is not something I can detest."

False Accusations, Scapegoating, Narcissism   Gaslighting, Normalizing

When finally, I became pregnant with my now precious daughter, I didn't tell him until I was nearly four months pregnant. I so wanted to share it and solicit some help from him to prevent another miscarriage. But I could never have handled the snide, verbal responses I had received. When I did summon the courage, he smiled sweetly but sneered, "Did you use the same donor? Maybe it will work again this time." I tried to explain it to myself knowing that I was hypersensitive about it and because of my changing hormones and, and, and… It didn't work. It hurt so badly.

We had been in the Adirondacks on vacation for two weeks and by now my clothes were far too tight. So, as soon as we arrived at home I said, "I'm going to the store to buy some maternity pants." He again smiled and said warmly, "Okay, the kids and I will unpack the car." On the way to the store I tried for the thousandth time to reconcile the vicious remarks and the warm kindness I had just experienced from the same man. I could not. We had enjoyed the two weeks in the mountains and the relaxation was delicious. After we returned, I went back to chastising myself with everything I could remember, rationalizing and making excuses for the difficult times I felt I(he) felt I had caused.

DT: Gaslighting, Goal posts always changing, Normalizing

False Accusations, Parental Alienation, Triangulation

Over the next few months, Brian had accepted a marketing call from realtors in the Pocono Mountains. The offer was pretty standard; a free weekend in the Poconos and a marketing tour in a new recreation community. When he told me, I could see how excited he was and suggested he tell his father that evening. The following day I asked my stepson if he had spoken with his father. He told me that they had called and made an appointment for some time in the near future. When I asked Dennis about the appointment and his intentions, it was obvious that I was doing so at the wrong time or in the wrong way as his expression became rigid and angry, "Oh, so now you are eavesdropping on my phone calls? I'll let you know when the plans are made."

For a long time, I had blamed a lot of the confusion and chaos on my own shortcomings.   Certainly, organizational skills were not my strong suit. However, I had been told and was aware that I did have good listening skills. On the other hand, I also knew that I was often distracted both by the daily demands made on me and the very real sense of the lack of reasonable communication. Every attempt I had made and, in every way, that I'd made the attempts to set aside a specific time for us to talk, Dennis sabotaged it. I was certain of that and knew that it was not my own failings or inability to accommodate. Neither was I now using one of his favorite dynamics of projecting the blame on to him. I took great care to do that and to re-examine both my motives and my methods of doing it.

DT: 13 Angry Dems, record numbers of WH staff leaving, Alienating allies, Canada. UK, Germany. NATO, etc.

Parental Alienation, Triangulation, Demeaning

The following Thursday afternoon, just before supper, I heard them talking about some fun things they were planning to do in the Poconos on the weekend coming. When he got home from work, I asked him about the weekend plans. "Oh, yeah, the appointment is this weekend to see the properties. Do you want to come?"

My first thought was "Not really. Not if I am just an extra" but I did not want to start that kind of angry conversation. So, I simply asked when we would leave and when we would return. There was a baby step forward at this point because I was fully aware that I had done nothing to provoke such treatment. It felt good to not go into the guilt and self-recrimination mode, but it also left me with absolutely no explanation. I felt adrift.

We went to the hotel the realtor had reserved on Friday night and the realtor came to meet us and make the appointment for Saturday morning. We drove around the recreation area for about an hour and then went back to the hotel for supper time. Saturday morning the realtor arrived early, and he did a thorough tour of the property and amenities. We asked some questions; the kids explored the amenities a bit and then we sat with the realtor exploring our priorities trying to match them with the available properties. The only input I really had was that I thought it would be wise to find the property close to the major amenities reducing the amount of transportation needed. The realtor marked his map with about five or six red checkmarks. We left to examine those properties. At one of them, a corner lot Dennis told the realtor that that was his favorite so far. They discussed the property a bit and Dennis told the realtor that that was the one we wanted. The realtor looked at me and said, "do you agree?" Dennis intervened and said, "sure, why wouldn't she?" The deal was done. I had nothing to say for the rest of the weekend. But the hurt and anger mounted, the confirmation of my non-importance was affirmed again, and I could find no solutions or options. For a short time, I tried to convince myself that I should be happy to be offered a vacation home. *I wasn'.t*

Belittling, Condescension, Triangulation

On one of the Sundays when his mother and brother came for dinner, they were in the living room with the children when I heard his mother saying to the children, "She's Irish and probably needs time to learn to cook and clean. But, maybe she will." Of course, I was offended, but more importantly, I thought it important that she support the efforts we were all making to form a new family. Dennis's reaction was only, "She doesn't understand any of that stuff." I answered "I believe she would but think it would be better received if it came from you rather than me No answer; no action.

Somewhere about 2 years into the marriage, Dennis told me that he would be late coming home after work one night a week for about six weeks. I assumed it was work- related and just asked, "should I have dinner for you when you get home?" "No, I'll have something **good** before I come home." What did that mean? He had only complained once about a meal I had made, ratatouille. I didn't like it either. Of course, neither did he ever expressed pleasure in the meals that I remember. I realized AGAIN that I was fearful of asking him why.

Six weeks later, he came home and handed me a very pretty pendant and chain. It was a blue oval stone in a lovely silver setting. There were 4 or 5 other unset stones as well. I admired them and asked, "Do you know what the stones are?"

"No, I wrote it down but left the list in the car." He said.

"Oh, where did you get them?"

"I made them at a rock polishing course I've been taking."

"Oh, is that where you've been going?"

He walked away angry saying,

"Yeah, but I don't answer to you."

"Of course not, but I'd like knowing that you are doing things you enjoy. I think of it more as sharing."

No response. Why would he not talk about his interests, projects, etc.?

The Morphing of an Honest Woman

The years of noncommunication, fear, contradictions, confusion and chaos lack of support, absence of affection, futile efforts to accommodate behaviors I could not understand and the chaos resulting from that left me empty, bereft, so confused that I had lost myself. I had lost MY SELF!!! There was a large part of me that was "disconnected, turned off". I went through each day just accomplishing tasks. I no longer expected pleasure, joy, happy events or anything very positive. I survived…I survived, I struggled, I hid. At a certain level, I still take a bit of pride in that. But looking back, there was a terrible sadness and loss involved. I still feel that it was beneficial for the children. But it certainly was destructive to me.

In the scant communication with him my goals had become SAFETY, avoidance of rages, distancing and protection of myself from him and the retention of what sanity I could. It started with avoidance and evasion. Most of my responses to his questions became, "I'm not sure, maybe, I'll find out, I'll let you know, etc.," I don't remember how long it took but soon my answers had become 100%

defensive. I was beyond able and no longer willing to risk the chaos and fear if I provided an unacceptable answer. And I most often did not know what would be unacceptable. It became similar to living in an alternate world. Truth became irrelevant, integrity was no longer a factor and honesty were absent. Survival, defensiveness, safety were now my primary goals.

Normalizing, Triangulation, False Accusations,

This became the norm and while very aware of that, I could find no safe alternatives. It went on throughout most of the rest of the "marriage". It obliterated anything close to intimacy. And it became a somewhat unknown norm in my own mind. In fact, it came into play once when I was working. I was working in international adoption and making a trip to Krasnoyarsk, Russia. At my layover in Moscow the customs officials did not believe that I was carrying as little cash as I had declared. They detained me for almost 48 hours. Did I feel threatened? Very much so. And I found it very easy to lie about the amount of cash I was carrying. Eventually, the customs officials became frustrated with me and told me to leave. The whole event was frightening in many ways; being detained, not knowing how it would be resolved, and seeing how easily it came to me to lie because I felt threatened.

One example of this that glared at me was that on the nights that I had fled my home and slept in the office; I do not think that Dennis knew where I was. I was not even sure that he cared. At some point, I stopped caring. When several of them had happened, I believe he became distressed, enraged or frantic, I don't know. But he began to call the office once it had opened in the morning, asking if I was there. When he was told that I was, he would feign relief, stating that I had not come home the night before. Another time he told our office manager that he was relieved because I had left the house in a condition that indicated that I should not drive. So, he just wanted to know that I was okay. After that had happened a couple of times, I heard myself telling the office manager that I had indeed gone home but had slept downstairs in order not to disturb him but had no idea how else I could handle things. Lying had become normalized. I did not even feel any sense of guilt or remorse or even any caring at all. I was safe. Looking back, I believe that this was the beginning of him trying to cast me in the light of the alcoholic he refused to acknowledge he was until he admitted that during our divorce.

Xxx We went up that weekend and met with the builder. It was totally clear that the deal was done. The builder did ask me what I thought of the design. As I went to answer, Dennis simply stated that I was not much into "energy efficiency." Humiliated again and realizing that any intervention on my part would only results in rage, I simply removed myself from the discussion. It is true that I had very little investment in what kind of house was built. And I also had not, up until that point been very energy aware. For me, that was not the issue. I wanted to be considered by my husband to be of some importance and some consequence.

DT: He has stopped giving press conferences, has fired any number of people through twitter rather than direct confrontation, James Comey found out he was fired on television, he more often than not uses surrogates to dispense information both to the public, his staff and other federal agencies. He held a summit with our most fierce adversary, Putin, behind closed doors and refuses to reveal the contents of that meeting.

Belittling, Demeaning, Narcissistic Supply, Normalization

About that time, I gave up trying. I had spent several years pondering, examining, blaming myself, feeling guilty, inadequate, alone and was continually self-recriminating. It was not a happy place to be, but I could see no options no matter what I had tried. I remembered the person I used to be vaguely; she was liked, loved, respected, and competent and happy. Even I had liked and loved her and felt a certain level of pride in who I was. I wanted that back! I wanted it back!

From about that time onward I simply became emotionally divorced from Dennis and in a very real way from myself. It was not something I wanted to do; I clearly knew I had to do it. I believe that was a turning point in my relationship with him, but more importantly in my relationship with my past self.

. "He is not mean; he is not bad; his disordered world is all he has. ...'

With that change, came a slight sense of freedom from the awful, continuous self-blame. I was more than willing to recognize that I had shortcomings, made mistakes, and was far less than perfect. But with the absence of communication and the continual, demeaning attitude, I could find no alternative. I could not discern what failings I had from that of the image projected by Dennis. The goal posts were always changing. And that is continually changing; one day he would complain that I was" incredibly controlling", another, he would mock my seeming inability to exert initiative. He complained continually about my incompetence, lying, failures, etc. it all became part of the hateful whole. Withdrawing from him did not resolve those feelings. But it did allow me to catch glimpses of who I used to be. That led to minor but meaningful feelings of hope.

It took some time but there was a gradual emancipation from the sadness, guilt, hurt, etc. and I began to free up my former self. Oh, how delicious that was. I developed a kind of mantra, and whenever he would rant/rage, I just withdrew to my mantra and waited for the end. Sometimes that was hours, sometimes weeks

. *"He is not mean; he is not bad; his disordered world is all he has. ...."*

"Living with or being involved with a narcissist can be mentally and emotionally exhausting. It can fee/ like you have to perform "mental gymnastics" from dealing with the lying (even when confronted with undeniable proof), the gaslighting, the triangulation, the projection, the constant contradictions, the manipulation, blame-shifting, the charm they lay on, the inflated sense of self- even subtle forms of torture, such as sleep deprivation, these people inflict on their victims - appears to be conscious and calculated to push the target of their "affections" past their limits, into surrender - and ultimately into total compliance - as a

Richard Skerrit   When Love is a Lie

As Dennis came closer to retirement age, I tried to talk with him a few times about his plans for retirement. He said his plan was to read and ski. When I responded that skiing was limited to only two or three months out of the year, he looked annoyed and simply said, "I know that, Marie." And left the room. Another issue that could have been unifying but, was isolating.

How alone he lived!

About two years later he was leaving for work one morning and said, "only one more week. I'll be finished with that train ride. I'll be finished with the whole crazy schedule." I asked what he meant, and he answered, "I'll be retired by the end of next week." He left. I was stunned. But not as stunned as I was a few weeks later. As he retired, there were several decisions he had made. One was how his pension would be distributed in case of his death. He could allocate the funds in three ways. While alive, he would receive 100% of his pension; in case of his death he could allocate either 75%, 50%, or 25% to his spouse. His choice would impact the amount of money he would receive each year depending on the percentage he had allocated for me. It was no surprise but certainly hurtful to find that he had allocated the lowest possible percentage for me in case of his death. When I stated that I would like to have been involved in that decision, he said, "why? The way you eat junk food, you'll have nothing to worry about." There is a terrible irony about the fact that I have already outlived him by 17 years. In truth, he was far more knowledgeable and diligent about eating well than I was and it still seems cruel that he did not really benefit from that.

About two years after my husband retired, I came home after work and found him, not surprisingly, in his recliner reading. Calling to him from the doorway I said, "Hi! How was your day?" He growled and sneered, "what the F… Do you care? Next to him on the floor I noticed our colander. He looked up at me with nothing short of hatred in his face and growled "Why the f… do we have a RED colander?" I hardly recognized this person as the man I had married. It was terrifying and repulsive to see that level of hate. My stomach tightened, I went on alert and my past experiences taught me what to do. He had fought a lifelong battle with depression, anxiety and other fiends. He had so valiantly fought that good fight. I feared now that he was losing it.

Since his retirement, it had become evident that the demons were winning.

As I looked at him now, I wavered between fear and painfully deep sorrow, I thought to explain that the red colander had been in the house before I married him. "Pointless", I thought," he's lost to me". His demons now dominated.

Over twenty-one years of marriage (non-marriage)I had learned the warning signs. I had also developed a safety routine for responding. I left the house and headed back to my office, a place of refuge, being careful to park in a secluded spot. I locked the doors to the office building behind me and used a small lamp in the middle part of the office so that the light would not be visible from outside. Whew! I felt safe. Safe, but so, so sad. For about six years I had kept a change of clothes and a small amount of cash in the trunk of my car and a toothbrush at the office. I had used them many times. During one of those years I had slept on the floor of my office 31 times and the frequency increased as the years went on. I had had Dennis arrested five times for assault and never wanted to do that to him or to me again. He never once asked me where I had been. But, then again, neither did I volunteer that information fearing that I would lose my safe place. I could not lose it and protecting it had become a primary concern of mine. I did hate the idea and in fact the reality of it but was crucial to my sense of safety.

During the early years, there was, of course, the matter of enough time. He rarely got home before 7:00pm from work, had finances to take care of, various repairs/projects in the house, etc. I was also busier than I had anticipated. So, one evening I said, "What would you think of a "date night" once a week? We could go locally to have coffee and dessert and have some time together." He very readily agreed and seemed pleased. "Is tonight a good night for our date?", I asked? "As good as any." We walked to a local diner and he surveyed the dessert display brightening when he saw the blueberry pie.

Silent Treatment, Self-aggrandizement

As we settled into a booth, I said, "I assume you are getting the blueberry pie." His answer was "you bet." He talked a good bit about what was happening at his job. "They could have built a better team; too many of them are new and don't have a good handle on the more intricate details. I could do this alone much faster." I was happy to hear about it even though much of it was too technical for me to understand. But I enjoyed getting to know some of how he felt about his work. While on that topic, I asked how long he had been working at his current job. He didn't exactly answer me but said that the only other full-time job he had had since college was for Western Union. He had left there because it wasn't big enough company for him "to grow in importance. He wanted room to spread his wings." I admired his ambition and confidence. We continued our "date night" for a few weeks and they were pleasant.

Years later, I learned that Western Union was indeed a very large and growing company. I never bothered to discuss that with him nor clarified the disparity between the facts and his perception of them.

A month or so later, I decided to make a blueberry pie as he seemed to enjoy it so much. When he finished dinner, I offered him a slice. He became agitated and almost screamed,

"I don't need those calories, I told you that."

"But you liked the one at Louie's so much..."

"That doesn't mean I want it every week! Don't you have any sense?"

He took the whole pie and threw it into the garbage.

"Dennis, the kids would like it and so would I." He was close to enraged and I knew it would be best to let it go, but it confounded me, so I added, "We have to figure out just what went on."

He left the kitchen, spent the night in the basement watching TV and refused to continue the date nights. The tension mounted, and the gulf widened.

What had provoked that level of anger? Did I say it wrong? Had he had a bad day at work? Was my timing poor? I spent hours, days pondering, reviewing, guessing. But I did not initiate any discussion because I was… Afraid!... Afraid!...Afraid! So much was fear and anger and almost no support, no forgiveness, acceptance, understanding, affection; and no communication or togetherness…no loving. To broach this with him would undoubtedly mean an argument, criticism, possible physical abuse and a long drawn out silent treatment again. I could not recall a single similar incident that resulted in better understanding, negotiating, compromise or resolution.

Emotional Abuse, Scapegoating, Anger.

The next morning, I had prepared his breakfast and the children had left for school. I wished him a good day on his way out. I frantically searched for a way to reach him and went to the front window to wave at him as he got into his car. Backing out of the driveway he waved back, and it signaled a wisp of hope…he didn't ignore me. BUT our neighbor across the street was backing out too and they had a slight collision. Both checked for damage and our neighbor drove off. Dennis pulled back into the driveway while I panicked and wished I were already dressed as I wanted desperately to run out of the house. As I feared, he came into the house and his rage was evident in his demeanor and expression. He immediately accused me of causing the accident because he had not come to bed the night before. Wisdom probably would have dictated my silence. But it was terror, fear, panic. I was immobilized, waited for the rant to end. During the rage, I was accused of retaliating against him, using bad judgment, plotting to hurt him and preventing him from performing his job **well**. ." I can't go to work and get things done when you provoke me like this!" Provoke him like what? Wave goodbye to him?

Normalization, Narcissism, Lack of Empathy

When he finally left for work, I did not feel the hurt; neither did I feel distressed; nor did I feel any impulse to work toward improving things. I simply felt hopeless, devalued, and numb. Looking back, it is almost bizarre that I simply went about the rest of the day without another thought about the event. I had accepted it as normal!!! NORMAL??! It had become just that, NORMAL!!!

I am one hundred percent Irish and from my early childhood St. Patrick's Day was always one of celebration, music, family and dancing. In the morning my sister and I would go with my father and march in the St. Patrick's Day parade. When we got home, we could smell the corned beef and cabbage and by then, there were family and friends beginning to gather. After dinner, we would roll up the rug in the living room and do Irish folk dancing. After I married Dennis, I continued celebrating St. Patrick's Day. The children's birth mother was Irish too and I felt they should know something of their Irish heritage. I would make corned beef and cabbage, play and Irish music and have a few shamrock decorations around the dining room. About the third or fourth St. Patrick's Day after I was married I did the same thing. When Dennis came home from work he looked a bit elated and said, "look what I bought!" He had brought home kielbasa and sauerkraut. So, I said, "Great for dinner for tomorrow will be very easy." "Tomorrow? I've been thinking about this all day. Let's have it now." "Dinner for today is already made." "But this doesn't take long. I've been looking forward to it." I was so hurt and so angry that I simply said, "Go ahead. We have our dinner and we're almost finished."

I knew by now that there was nothing that we shared., and nothing he wanted to share. But, I continually searched for reasons within myself thinking, "I have to work harder to find an interest of his to share, I haven't tried to learn much about the technical field he works in, I should get more involved in the Humanist society", etc. It took me days to accept that I held no fault this time. It was good to realize that, but it also meant that I had to face the fact that no amount of adaptation on my part would lead to "a marriage".

Triangulation, Alienation

Another issue that concerned me was that the three children rarely spent time together. They course, were each four years apart in age. But I still felt they would benefit from time together. They each had a television in their own room and after supper and homework went to their own rooms and watched TV. When one of the TVs needed to be replaced, I suggested to Dennis that it might be worth considering buying just one larger TV and putting it in the basement family room. He of course, questioned me as to why. I explained that it would give to three children more time to be together, an opportunity to learn to share, compromise and it might develop memories for them for their futures.

Within a few days, Dennis came home with one TV to replace the one that had broken. No discussion. <u>No recognition that I was in the role of stepparent.</u>

There was an occasion where we all went to a summer festival in northern New Jersey. It was an annual event and had entertainment and events for all ages. When lunchtime came we all went to one of the picnics tables and started to look again at the program. As we were doing that Dennis looked down at my feet and saw that I had two different socks on. Both socks were white and very similar. However, he got very upset pointed out to the children that I had miss matched socks and insisted that we leave so that "no one else would notice." I was dumbfounded but none of the children seemed surprised. In fact, on the way home they lately teased me about it. Everyone but me seemed to feel it was a major infraction. It took me too long to understand how obsessive his perfectionism was.

Later that week I went to Eddy's room to put laundry away. The door was standing open and just before entering I looked and saw a very large, snake on the floor. I firmly closed the door, went downstairs, and called the police. I wanted that snake removed immediately. When the police came, they identified the snake as a boa constrictor, estimated the weight as 35 to 40 pounds and confirmed my fear that it could definitely be lethal. They had brought a cage, put the snake into it and I sat and trembled for about two hours. Only days before that and I told the older children that their little sister was becoming mobile and they should put everything important out of her reach. Was Eddy using poor judgment? Was it a sadistic gesture? Was there any other explanation? In either case, this had to be addressed immediately, decisively, and effectively.

I spent the rest of the day trying to decide how to handle the event. The relationship between Eddy and Dennis was mostly contentious. There had been several times when I had stood between the two of them as their arguments had become physical assaults.

Anger, Scapegoating, Dissociation

That evening when I told Dennis about the event, the expected rage occurred. He screamed, "you're always picking on Eddy. Stop lying about what he does." I simply handed him the copy of the police report and the receipt for the snake which I had found on Eddy's bureau. I took my daughter and went to a nearby motel. Not feeling very proud of it, I got a small pleasure from handing Dennis's credit card to the clerk.

Over the next few months, I again just adapted…mostly silence, sadness, avoidance, and more sadness. To date, I was responsible for his Eddy's tattoos (which he had before I met him), the water in the basement (because I did too much laundry!), his late arrival at work that "ruined my record and reputation", Eddy's experiment with LSD, his own loneliness, the death of the motor of the power drill, his second son's ADD, all other problems he could attribute to "poor diet", the pealing dining room ceiling paint, etc., etc. He refused to address any of these and no matter how I tried, there was a tirade and threats and I often had to leave the house for safety.

"He is not mean, he is not bad; his disordered world is all he has.; he is doing his best; his best, his best, is not something I can detest."

I did not understand for several years and only with gradual awakening. This disorder left him with an overwhelming TERROR of failure or being seen as less than perfect. He **needed** a scapegoat. It was not conscious or deliberate and he knew of no other way of living. Therefore, he created, for his own survival, a woman he perceived as hateful and he hated her. I lived with a good man who I had loved but now feared??? When this realization began to take shape, it was clearer why nearly every woman in his life was described as hateful. Yet, I did have very real evidence that I was liked, trusted, respected, competent, etc. everywhere else in my life. I had had a loving, close knit family of origin, I had had and still have many very long-term friendships, I had the respect of colleagues, and enjoyed many, varied relationships with acquaintances and neighbors.

Now, where do I go from here?

I again suggested that I join him at his next appointment with his psychiatrist, but, did so halfheartedly. There just seemed no avenue of communication; maybe a mediator would help. I could recall NO time when a difference was resolved through compromise, negotiation, or discussion. He sought only to place blame.

He was definitely not happy about the suggestion, but, agreed.

During the session, he continually raised issues other than our relationship; Eddy's problematic behavior, his negative relationships at work, his concerns about his cousins in Queens whom he referred to as his "beer guzzling" cousins, etc. His doctor repeatedly brought the conversation back to the marriage. But he never engaged. After the session, I made an excuse to do an errand and realized that I was afraid to go home. When I got home, he was asleep in the basement.

DT: no matter how major or minor the national issue is, as is documented, he deflects all issues to HIM and in many of those issues this focus becomes his victimization. For example: the fake news depicts him poorly, the criticism of the management of the hurricane in Puerto Rico, he converts into his suffering and victimization and claims it is an unsung success, he often questions why he is not praised enough were given enough credit. Even the recent issue of the serious and significant failure to care for those devastated in hurricane Maria, he focused on how great he had been, what a magnificent job his administration had done and how HIS success had been an unsung success.

ANDY

Scapegoating, Anger, Projection, Imposed Isolation, Abuse, Disassociation

April always brought me a sense of hope and anticipation. This was true in April 1982 as well. That year I had planned a surprise fiftieth birthday party for my husband for early May.

He had a family of cousins in Queens, whom we rarely saw. On a lovely day at the end of April my husband, our daughter drove to his mother's home in Queens to take her to dinner for her birthday. I had suggested that we invite his cousins as well. He simply ignored the suggestion. His brother joined us as he had recently been laid off from his job as a graphic artist. It was evident during the dinner that

Andy was much less interested in his meal than usual and scarcely spoke. When we returned to his mother's house Andy brought his brother to the basement to look at some of the oil paintings he had done in the past. He urged my husband to bring some of them back to our home for hanging. My husband declined.

On the ride, back home I noted to my husband that Andy had hardly eaten, seemed very withdrawn, and had attempted to give away some of his most prized possessions. (I am a psychiatric Social Worker) The symptoms of depressed appetite, disposal of personal possessions, withdrawal from social interaction and the loss of employment sounded frighteningly like the classic pre-suicide symptoms. Those symptoms together with the knowledge that Andy had made a suicide attempt about fifteen years earlier prompted me to act with some sense of urgency. When I spoke of it to my husband, he became agitated and accused me again of being "the voice of doom". I understood his resistance to accepting this and made unsuccessful attempts to approach this topic gently during the next two days. But I also knew that the symptoms were too explicit, too definitive and far too serious to ignore or accept his deflection of the responsibility onto me.

On Wednesday of the following week my mother-in-law called our house obviously in great distress. She had reverted to speaking her native language, so I put my husband on the phone immediately. She explained to him that Andy had not come home for 72 hours. This had never happened before. My husband attempted to reassure her that this was not a cause for great concern. After he hung up and told me why his mother had called serious alarms sounded in my brain. I offered to go to my mother-in-law's home to stay with her and comfort her. At first, my husband discouraged me stating that in her old age his mother was prone to mildly hysterical reactions. After a few hours, I convinced him that I should go even if only to offer support and companionship. In this serious situation I had to call on the qualities that my "old self" had confidence left in.

I took my three-year-old daughter and a few of our belongings and drove to my mother-in-law's house. Seeing her when I arrived, I knew that I had done the right thing. She was more distraught than I had anticipated. We looked all through the house, the property and nearby areas. We even walked up to the local park and searched there. There was no sign of Andy anywhere.

To my surprise, when I suggested we call the police and file a missing person report. my mother-in-law very readily accepted the opportunity for help in finding her son. However, when I did call the police, they understandably expected that a 52-year-old bachelor might well not be expected to be at home every night. They declined to accept the missing person report. I took two pictures of Andy and went back to the local police station to try to explain that there were extenuating circumstances. The report was accepted and completed at the police precinct and they committed to making what search they could. I was not convinced that they saw this as urgent. When I returned to my mother-in-law, she was verging on hysteria and had again reverted to speaking her native language. For two more days, we thought, worried and tried in vain to develop a theory as to where Andy might be.

As the weekend approached, I explained to my mother-in-law that we needed to go back to my home in New Jersey as my three stepchildren would need me. Although she agreed, she found endless reasons to forestall the departure. The last reason was that she had left some wood in the garage and wanted to bring it for use in our fireplace. I offered to get the wood as she got into the car. She gave me the garage key and I raised the door. Near the front of the garage and to my horror I saw my brother-in-law who had hung and castrated himself. Immediately, I pulled the door down trembling. I went back to the car and told my daughter that we had enough time for her to watch Mr. Rogers and I brought her and my mother-in-law back into the house. In the kitchen and explained that I had found Andy in the garage but that he had died there. She seemed dazed and asked no questions as she sat there absorbing the information while I dialed the police.

When the police arrived, my mother-in-law was weeping but had asked no questions. Because I was still holding the garage keys the police began to question me as a murder suspect. Happily, they seemed to quickly grasp the situation. The next hours are a blur to me. I remember the police taking pictures in the garage and asking questions. I remember the coroner vehicle arriving and seeing the body removed in a body bag.

When I had called my husband at work to tell him that we had found his brother, he had questions but all I told him was that Andy had passed away. He stated that he would be there within an hour. When he did arrive, he angrily accused me of being heartless and cruel stating that death should never be a message delivered by phone. He hit me hard knocking my head into the side of the house. Looking back, I could almost laugh remembering that he said, "Next time my brother dies, don't dare tell me over the phone". A police officer quickly came and accused him of assault. When the officer learned he was my husband he accepted that no charges would be pressed.

When my husband spoke with the police and learned the details of his brother's death, he then accused me of reveling in the "pleasure" of being correct about my predictions for his brother. All this I attributed to the trauma he must be experiencing.

Andy's wake and funeral were painfully sad. The only attendees at the wake were immediate family members and one high school friend who had not seen Andy in what he estimated was about fifteen years. I think a few neighbors stopped by. In addition, the wake was held on Mother's Day which was also my husband's 50th birthday. The anniversaries of both those events imposed anguished memories for all the years to come. No need to state that he also had a problem expressing his anger constructively.

DT:: Obama left a mess, Hillary caused it, the Fake News is hurting me, the Mueller investigation is interfering with my ability to perform my duties as president; no respect or value placed in the value of the first amendment, all of his declarations about the Mueller investigation being a hoax, rigged, illegal, in spite of the documented 4000 lies he told during his first year and a half as president; well, those are alternative facts.

During the following weeks, there was a pall over the family. Although I tried to encourage Dennis and the children to talk to each other about the event, the only emotion I saw was Brian's anger. He was clearly very upset, punched a hole in the wall in his room and was sullen, angry and distressed for several weeks.

Frankly, his reaction seemed more in keeping with the normal standards I would have expected. At least, he reacted. That was beyond anything I saw in the other three members of the family.

My feelings were sadness of course, some guilt that I had not acted more forcefully and earlier, and a strange sense of confusion and bewilderment. But that had become not only familiar, but standard operating procedure. During that time, I felt unable to process my reactions to the entire event. I cannot claim that I felt a sense of loss for Andy as I had never been able to form a relationship with him. My most poignant feelings were pain for my family members but a definite disconnect from them as the issue seemed to not to be one for sharing or discussion.

Several weeks later I was doing laundry in the basement when, for no apparent reason, the overhead light went out. I had always thought of the family room in the basement as Andy's room since he stayed there when his mother and he babysat for the children. The light going out so suddenly, struck me with terror and all I could do was run back upstairs and keep running. I ran to the next town, turned around and ran back, probably 4-5 miles. I was breathless, trembling and perspiring. I knew that these reactions were to more than the long run. I needed help.

A couple of weeks later I made an appointment with my husband's psychiatrist. I did not feel that the recent events were something I wanted to burden a friend with. But now I knew I needed help to manage my reactions. As I spoke with the psychiatrist, I could literally feel the burden being lifted a bit. He recognized the traumatic dimension and offered some support. He also shared with me that he expected none would be available from my husband. My response was that I did not feel my husband should be supporting me, but he also sought and accepted no support from me. I felt I should be supporting him and did not expect any from him. But Dennis accepted none of my offers of support. I assumed that he was just not ready. The doctor told me that none would be coming from him in any case. He, in fact, was incapable of giving and receiving any empathy or compassion. When I questioned him, his response was that my husband had a severe narcissistic personality disorder in addition to his chronic depression. He was incapable of compassion or empathy. He felt he could and should share this with me as we had both come for counseling regarding our marriage and were therefore seen by him as one patient.

While this news was as devastating as the prior weeks had been, it did help me to understand the past years since my "marriage", e.g. why my husband had never picked me up from the hospital after my several miscarriages, why he had not attended the funeral of our child who had died, why he came to the hospital only when I begged when my sister learned she had breast cancer and needed a mastectomy claiming that we had made plans to go to the house in the Poconos for that Memorial Day weekend and he really wanted to go. I simply stated that I would not be going to the Poconos. He did come to the hospital, but we drove in separate cars so that he could leave for the Poconos directly from there. He stayed a short time, was pleasant, made his excuses and left the hospital. I did not hear from him for the rest of the weekend and he had no questions about my sister's condition when he returned. At that time, it was considered that if the cancer had not spread or if there was no evidence that it had metastasized, you were considered "cured". My sister's family and I celebrated greatly on the four-year anniversary. Dennis declined to join stating that he felt we were being naïve and overly optimistic. Unfortunately, he was correct. Shortly after the celebration it was discovered that the cancer had indeed metastasized and had affected her pancreas, liver, and blood. She began to decline significantly and somewhat rapidly. During that time, her husband found that there was a nasty leak in the ceiling their room which had to be repaired immediately. I, of course agreed that she could stay with us during the repair time. Her son, my nephew, was on the volunteer ambulance corps in his town. He arranged to have her brought to my home in a comfortable way. She was with us for about a week and a half and I cherished that time with her.

I had both Dennis and me out of our room and moved to the basement. Our room was by far the most comfortable place for her. I did not consult with Dennis and did not care what his feelings were. For several years after her death, Dennis would go on periodic rages about how selfish, inconsiderate, and deceptive I was about that.

"He is not mean; he is not bad; his disordered world is all he has. He's doing his best; his best is not something I can detest."

When the ceiling repair was completed, my nephew again brought his mother back home. While she was semi-comatose during the time, she was with me, we did have lucid time when we talked about so many things, resolve the few differences that lingered, and came together in a way I am so deeply grateful for.

I never tried to share this with Dennis fearing that, as with so many positive things, he would have disparaging, negative responses. I did not want him to touch this.

But a few times during the following years, he did refer to that time again as me "manufacturing a false need to have my way."??? Why he never allowed me to be involved in any financial aspect, why he made no effort to respect my wish to be married in the Catholic Church, why there was never any reflection/discussion about our sex life, etc. Why I was always so alone? Why was there never any "us"?

"He is not mean, he is not bad; his disordered world is all he has.; he is doing his best; his best, his best, is not something I can detest."

Several over the next year,

Narcissism, Anger, False Accusations, Triangulation, Dissociation

A few months after Andy's suicide his cousin called and, as usual, only asked for him, but, then said" Oh, Marie, I want you to know that we forgive you." When I asked my husband what I was being forgiven for, he replied that it was for causing Andy's suicide, as I had not given Andy a 50th birthday party as I had planned to do for Dennis!!

As painful as that was to hear, it was the inauguration of my emancipation. This was so obviously the product of "disordered" thinking that it began to free me from the endless plaguing of searching for my failures, my fears, my guilt, my inadequacies, etc.

<u>EMANICIPATION</u>

I cannot emphasize too much the explanation for the continual lying; it bears repeating. A person with narcissistic personality disorder has a wound so deep and so painful that their defense against anything that **<u>they perceive</u>** to be threatening, **requires** that they reject that reality, reconstruct it to reduce the terror they feel about the perceived threat. This can literally occur moment to moment and can reverse itself just as quickly. Following that, they require those in their immediate environment to confirm and accept the reconstructed reality. Obviously, this creates incredible confusion and chaos as they are unaware that they are doing it in those with them obviously do not know what the newly constructed reality is. It obliterates any possibility of togetherness on any level. It also explains the continuous confusion and chaos and the resulting exhaustion.

Some examples are given above but it seems expedient to briefly reiterate some of them; the time his son experimented with LSD, the time his son had bought and released a boa constrictor, the two times his son had used Dennis's car without permission, damaged it slightly and Dennis blamed me for both events, etc.

All of the times that I tried to present Dennis with behaviors that were of great concern to me, he behaved with rage, ramps, threats and behaviors that were completely incomprehensible to me. And I also knew in most instances that he was absolutely incorrect. But there was no option to try to negotiate, explain or resolve the difference because <u>he could not tolerate those truths.</u> Therefore, **his reality became that I was the liar.**

And the horror I was that I did. At least, one of the "fractured parts" of me did and soon I began to detest, even deny, that part of me. I began to conduct my life outside of my home and at a safe distance from all those in my home. This was not a conscious decision and is not one I am proud of.

I never was able to find a way to live with that dichotomy and for the most part, I simply separated myself from him in every way I could. But the cost of that was exceedingly high. I despised myself severely yet could not find an alternative way of retaining myself and still remain safe. That damage remains even until today. I had always liked who I was, not a perfect person, but a good one. Now I basically detested the person I was at home. That was why beginning to work was so important and supported my attempts to retain the part of me that I could like. That was what the therapist had meant by saying that my ego was "fractured".

In addition, there were coworkers and new friends also confirmed that I was likable. That may sound shallow, but at the time, it was enormously nurturing and confirming.

DT: the size of his inaugural crowds were bigger than ever before; the accusations that James Comey was a liar, the claims that the entire WH staff had adequate clearances, the statements that he would release his tax returns and withdraw from administering his businesses, etc. these and other lies have been documented to be more than 12,000.

His endless disparaging statements about other world leaders, our own intelligence community, members of his own administration, clearly alienated many of them from him and divided our government. The divisions grew exponentially.

Now, the New York Times op-ed release, the Bob Woodward book "fear" and now the Paul Manafort agreement have given innumerable additional examples.

<u>The Morphing of an Honest Woman</u>

The years of noncommunication, fear, contradictions, lack of support, absence of affection, futile efforts to accommodate behaviors I could not understand and the chaos resulting from that left me empty, bereft, so confused that I had lost myself.

In the scant communication with him my goal had totally become safety, avoidance of rages, distancing myself from him and the retention of what sanity I could. It started with avoidance and evasion. Most of my responses to questions became, "I'm not sure, maybe, I'll find out, I'll let you know, etc.," I don't remember how long it took but soon my answers had become 100% defensive. I was beyond able and no longer willing to risk the chaos if I provided an unacceptable answer. And it was impossible to know what would be unacceptable as it changed relative to his mood. Truth became irrelevant, integrity was no longer a factor and honesty were absent. Survival, defensiveness, were now my primary goals.

"Living with or being involved with a narcissist can be mentally and emotionally exhausting. It can feel like you have to perform "mental gymnastics" from dealing with the lying (even when confronted with undeniable proof), the gaslighting, the triangulation, the projection, the constant contradictions, the manipulation, blame-shifting, the charm they lay on, the inflated sense of self- even subtle forms of torture, such as sleep deprivation, these people inflict on their victims - appears to be conscious and calculated to push the target of their "affections" past their limits, into surrender - and ultimately into total compliance - as a source of Narcissistic Supply". *Richard Skerrett "When Love is a Lie".*

One example of this that glared at me was that on the nights that I had fled my home and slept in the office; I do not think that Dennis knew where I was. I did not really think that he cared. When several of them had happened, I believe he became curious, distressed or frantic, I don't know. But he began to call the office once it had opened asking if I was there. When he was told that I was, he would feign relief, stating that I had not come home the night before, thus, implying that I was either having an affair or doing something nefarious. Another time he told our office manager that he was relieved because I had left the house in a condition that indicated that I should not drive. So, he just wanted to know that I was okay. After that had happened several times, I heard myself telling the office manager that I had indeed gone home but had slept downstairs in order not to disturb him. "Oh, what a tangled web we weave." I was ashamed of the lies but had no idea how else I could handle things. Looking back, I believe that this was the beginning of him trying to cast me in the light of the alcoholic he refused to acknowledge himself to be. The plot thickened.

Gaslighting

This is a very important, subtle and insidious dynamic used by those with narcissistic personality disorder. They need it and use it in order to confirm for themselves that their disordered world reality is broader than their own interior world. As they convince others that their reality is real, others begin to behave in that way, and it confirms the disordered reality for everyone. How serious and destructive that is for someone who is in power.

As I have come to learn, it is far more dangerous than I realized for a long time. Those who are being gaslighted are experiencing the same chaos, confusion and exhaustion that I had been feeling. Obviously, they cannot perform their responsibilities effectively.

I would strongly recommend that anyone reading this book consider watching the free Amazon movie from the 1940s named "Gaslight."

Any number of times I can remember Dennis correcting me, denigrating me in the presence of the children. I found it wrong, repulsive, destructive as well as hurtful. But, for far too long I manufactured all sorts of excuses for him, often tried to discuss it with him. It only led to rants and rages; never negotiating, compromise or improvement of any sort, never!

But as time went on it became more hurtful and destructive and my only option seemed to be to distance myself from him. That was just as destructive in another way.

What I missed, was how I had been and was being gaslighted myself. For years I had a confidence in what he said and accepted a good deal of it is true. It took me so long to realize how harmful it had been.

As a child I had seen an off-Broadway show named "Scapegoat" but was too young to transfer that information to my current situation. Had I been able to share this with my sister, friends, or any support system it might have been very enlightening and productive. However, this system in place in the house was alienation from almost anyone and everyone. My support system had been alienated.

Gaslighting, as described in the symptom descriptions is "the practice of brainwashing or convincing a mentally healthy individual that they are going insane or that their understanding of reality is mistaken or false."

I had begun to believe that many of his colleagues were dumb, naïve, lazy, and ineffective. Similarly, I had accepted that much of what he said about the women in his past life was factual. For far too long, I believed so many negative things that he had said about members of the society he was a member of, neighbors, his relatives and almost all those in his life. It even got to the point where I bought into with and his feelings of victimization to the extent that I was empathizing with him and trying to make suggestions so that he might have more satisfying relationships.

Far too late but, eventually my realities won out. I am both grateful and indebted to my wonderful parents who were very committed to having their daughters learn to do critical thinking. That was what led to a decision that probably saved my sanity.

As I began to identify the gaslighting and the alienation and lying (distorting of reality), it became readily clear that I must seek normalcy. Normalcy! Even the word brought consolation.

The children were becoming more independent and I look to the local community to find some setting in which I could find a different standard against which I could get a reflection of a broader understanding and reflection of who I was.

It began with going to a local town Council meeting which turned out to be contentious to an exaggerated degree. That was not a setting in which I could find anything which I thought would be helpful. I had more than enough of that at home.

On the way out of the meeting I noticed a note on a bulletin board which announced a Tupperware party only blocks from my home. It crossed my mind that there might at least be some neighbors going to that party and with whom I might find some compatibility.

Little did I know where that Tupperware party would lead!

At the party was a woman, a neighbor who had very recently returned from South America having adopted a beautiful little girl. Adoption had been a significant part of my life for years; my sister had adopted three children;

my parents had informally adopted several children who needed temporary care. The adoptive mother and I struck up a quick friendship and realized that both of our daughters were very close in age. We planned for them to play together and the results still amaze me.

The other woman was anxious to supplement her income, wanted to work part-time and of course now had an intense interest in adoption. Within a few weeks, we had decided to apply to be licensed as an adoption agency to do only two adoption services which could be done evenings. It took about a year to accomplish that but during that process I had contact with a variety of people, gotten positive feedback from them and my self-confidence was redeveloping. And the normalcy of those contacts was nourishing, supportive, constructive.

Because my partner in the agency had recently adopted, she was in touch with a very active adoptive parent support group, the Latin American Parents Association and very quickly we began to have referrals from them. As our clientele began to increase. I tried to explain to Dennis what our work entailed but he had no interest whatsoever. The major portion of our work was doing pre-adoption homestudy evaluations for families who are hoping to adopt. At first, it was very unappealing, and I felt like an inspector. But the contact with normal couples was so beneficial to me personally that I never hesitated to continue.

Harassment, Disparagement and Threats

Soon Dennis began to refer to me as a "toilet counter". And I will readily admit that once or twice I was tempted to retort, "it's better than a bean counter." But I had never wanted that kind of mean exchange and therefore, for the thousandth time, I bit my tongue. He would make the remarks snidely and grin. It could happen several times daily. Over the years we developed placement programs in several countries and eventually placed just over two thousand children from third world countries. He retained the denigrating nick name "toilet counter" missing all the joy and gratification. More sadness!

Of course, it hurts but my major reaction was to pity him through that level of anger. My new work was filled with joy, normalcy, and a large measure of success. He was completely unable to enjoy any of that. I did sometimes wonder if he felt a level of competition with me and maybe resented the success. But there was nothing I was willing to do about that.

DT: His main focus from the beginning of his campaigning and through his presidency to date has been to demean, denigrate and criticize Obama. He has never been able to feel satisfied that he has obliterated Obama adequately. Yet he still has no insight as to why this is an isolating approach and he is still very much alone in his pursuit of success.

Within about a year or year and a half our client volume had increased and a larger and larger number of reports needed to be written. I was vaguely aware of word processing but had no real idea what that meant. A little research revealed that it was exactly what we needed to do.

Because Dennis worked with an IT department, I considered asking him for some guide. Very quickly I realized that that was extremely unwise and would be fruitless. He did hear me talking on the phone about wanting to learn more about word processing and the following day he brought me home one of the new computer magazines.

He pointed out that in that magazine was a full word processing program, but it needed to be typed onto a floppy disk. I have never been, and still am not, even an intermediate typist. The agency did have a superb typist who was more than willing to do that.

For the next several weeks my super typist and I sat at the computer and learned one of the very early programs for word processing. Between the two of us we made rather rapid progress. And that set us on the track for developing the agency even more.

Dennis, did at one point, walk past us, put his hand on my shoulder and with the big smile said, "Ah, two toilet counters". My typist happily was too engrossed in learning our new skill and I happily don't believe she even heard it.

A few weeks later Dennis was on his way to a committee meeting and asked me if I would print an envelope for a letter, he was giving to one of the members. I explained that I had not yet learned to do envelopes but would try and bring it to him if I was successful. It took about an hour, but the envelope was done. I brought him two of them just in case he would need them.

Bringing him the envelopes I tried to be as unobtrusive as possible as the meeting was in progress. But when I entered the room, he looked up and said loudly, "Oh, my favorite toilet counter is here!". I was both embarrassed and angry. When I looked at the other members on the committee, they looked embarrassed as well as confused.

I wanted so much to talk to him about how he "shot himself in the foot" repeatedly with that kind of talk. It was so obviously self-defeating and self-destructive. But I knew where a talk like that would lead and I simply let it go. We both lost.

Projection, Imposed Isolation, Relationship Hyper Vigilance

About two years after my husband retired, I came home after work and found him, not surprisingly, in his recliner reading. Calling to him from the doorway I said, "Hi! How was your day?" Next to him on the floor I noticed our colander. He looked up at me with nothing short of hatred in his face and growled "Why the f... do we have a RED colander?" I hardly recognized this person as the man I had married. It was terrifying and repulsive to see that level of hate. My stomach tightened, I went on alert and my past experiences taught me what to do. He had fought a lifelong battle with depression, anxiety and other fiends. He had so valiantly fought that good fight. I feared now that he was losing it.

Since his retirement, it had become evident that the demons were winning.

As I looked at him now, I wavered between fear and painfully deep sorrow. I thought to explain that the red colander had been in the house before I married him. "Pointless", I thought, "he's lost to me". His demons now dominated.

Over 21 years of marriage I had learned the warning signs. I had also developed a safety routine for responding. I left the house and headed back to my office, a place of refuge, being careful to park in a secluded spot. I locked the doors to the office building behind me and used a small lamp in the middle part of the office so that the light would not be visible from outside. Whew! I felt safe. Safe, but so, so sad. For about six years I had kept a change of clothes and a small amount of cash in the trunk of my car and a toothbrush at the office. I had used them many times. During one of those years I had slept on the floor of my office 31 times and the frequency increased as the years went on. I had had Dennis arrested five times for assault and never wanted to do that to him or to me again.

And on it went. In addition, I was becoming what I now know is a hypervigilant personality. Always on alert to his moods, sensitivities, needs; I never felt safe or at peace when he was home. That meant that I was almost always preoccupied with evaluating his moods, his needs, and the potential dangers that might arise from saying or doing the wrong thing.

IAM

At some point, I have no idea when, it began; a brief, dream/fantasy of me walking alone down a long, endless desert road with no traffic, no color, no settlements, no vegetation, nothing other than brown. There seemed to be no destination or purpose and no beginning or end. Walking was very deliberate, slow-paced and yet felt pointless. Early on, the fantasy might occur every few weeks. But within months it took up residence and presented itself often during the day, but frequently during the night. On some low-level of consciousness, I it was clear that this was a depiction of how I saw my life. It was too frightening to actually look at it.

I also remember a few times, walking along the main street in our town, passing several store windows and catching a glimpse of a woman that looked familiar. I stopped and turned around but could not see her. When I turned again and faced the store window, she was back. It took three tries before I realized that I was looking at myself but not recognizing her. That was indeed frightening.

Narcissistic was a term I was informed about, but what I missed, was the **FULL** meaning of personality DISORDER. His disordered world was his only reality for him. And, I was not a valid player in that world, except as a tool and scapegoat. I had no reality for him. That was so devastating, demeaning and painful to realize. What was I doing here? He didn't even care enough to hate me? In fact, he didn't even know me or care to. A few times I approached him about the mounting tension and lack of affection, suggesting a separation. Those suggestions were, at first triggers for a "truce", a period of calm, but not one for resolving or even defining issues and they lasted for shorter and shorter periods.

Threatening

One of those times, I was making a costume for a school event for my daughter. The plethora of prior events was crowding in on me as was the meaning of them and I had begun to cry. Dennis came into the room and told me he was going on an errand and did not know what time he would return. I didn't care. I looked at him and said that I needed a separation and could not continue to live like this. He picked up the iron I was using and placed it on his forehead saying "you aren't going anywhere; believe me I will not permit that.

Then, suddenly I knew clearly that this was not a life I could continue. There was a clarity about that. I knew that I needed to put an end to this.

Summoning all the courage I could and staring down the fear, I approached Dennis and trying desperately to not imply any blame to him, I stated, "Dennis, I am so sorry, but I am too unhappy to continue living this way." Instantly, the rage appeared, I panicked, and he said, "you're always complaining. You're never happy. Well, if you're willing to accept responsibility for the death of the father of four, remember you will have to live with that. You will have to live with that with the rest of your life." Later that evening he walked into the bedroom, handed me an empty medicine bottle and laid down on the floor. I actually hesitated for a couple of moments before I called the ambulance. When the ambulance came, they asked me what medication he had taken. I had not even looked at the bottle. And I could not answer their question about how much medication had been in bottle. Now I felt narcissistic. My mind would not move off the question, "What can I do now? What can I do now?" For that few moments I hadn't the strength to even care about how much danger he was in.

After a short time, I went over to the hospital, waited for him not even asking for a medical report. I drove him home in silence. I still don't know if that was a "gesture" a threat, or an attempt. It was irrelevant as there was nothing I could do for him. He had no relationship with me.

He moved out of the bedroom that night. All I felt was relief, relief, relief.

On one occasion, a friend called and told me her husband was having car trouble and needed a ride home from about 5-6 miles away. She asked if I could either babysit or pick him up. I left a note for Dennis, went to pick up her husband and returned home within about a half hour. Returning, I noticed that all lights were out and felt relief that I could have some peace for the evening. When I entered the house, I saw Dennis in the corner of the dining room in his underwear holding a large corning ware bowl. He yelled out at me that he knew that I had met my boyfriend for drinks AGAIN and I had no right to come back to **HIS** house. He threw the bowl at me, missed and lunged at me. He was again very drunk, and I was so frightened. I slipped away and left the house. I had NEVER been unfaithful to him in any way, didn't drink at all and knew I needed help, support?

False Accusations

Again, I had NEVER been unfaithful to him in any way, didn't drink at all and could make no sense of any of it. More and more that thought hovered in my mind "could make no sense of it." More confusion, more chaos, and more severe sadness.

Walking the mile or so to my office, it simply became clearer that this had to end; it was not even a decision but simply a realization. The exhaustion was beyond anything I had ever known. At some point I became aware that I was feeling very cold and wet and woke up to find myself asleep under a tree in a local park and it was raining. That day I made an appointment with a psychiatrist/therapist to try to clarify my options, find some support and hopefully begin to resolve the whole painful issue.

After several sessions with the psychiatrist, she tried to have me formulate a plan based on my priorities. It was stunning to hear myself say that I still cared about him and the children and wanted to do everything I could to preserve the family. I could not say that I loved him. But having seen how he sabotaged almost every relationship he had and how alone he was and how much he was hurting I could not contribute additional pain by leaving him. She pushed me hard to try to enumerate and explain what I thought might be effective and what I had tried. Brick wall. For about half an hour I listed all the efforts I had made, all hopes I had relinquished, all the failed attempts. She came over and stood behind my chair putting her hands on my shoulders in an incredibly comforting gesture. It was at least an hour before I could stop crying. No, before I could stop sobbing.

She stayed next to me, very patiently waiting and at just the right moment she said, "we have some hard work to do, Marie. Let me know if you need some more time, to begin now or what the best thing is for you to do for yourself." I heard it all and appreciated it but when she said, "to do for yourself", I panicked. Real panic! For myself? Who was me? I didn't know anymore. The fantasy recurred but this time I was running at great neck speed down that bleak road, but I was invisible. I saw no one running anywhere; no destination, no signs and no indications that there would be an end. I relayed the fantasy to her, explained its origin, and was left with a frantic need to find the person who used to be and who I liked and needed to find. "Please help me find her. Please. I need her again." The psychiatrist so beautifully reassured me. She also stated, "Marie, I believe your husband has a severe narcissistic personality disorder. It's not curable." And then a piece of invaluable advice. "If you feel hateful, and you very well may, try to hate the disease, not him. Hosting hate will do you great harm and you do not deserve that." I was not really able to hear that then. But in the months and years to come I came to deeply appreciate it.

IM

My Invisible Me became a more frequent visitor. She was not friendly or unfriendly; not judgmental nor supportive, she was neither happy nor sad, there were no characteristics about her that I could name. She just was. I did give her a nickname: IM. Then the irony struck me. On the one hand, her nickname was extremely impersonal; on the other hand, when pronounced, it was I am. An attempt at affirming my reality? I am., I am. Her presence was felt randomly; sometimes two or three times a day; sometimes not for weeks. I was indifferent about the frequency; but had a vague hope that she would remain although I don't know why.

A few times I wondered if IM was similar to an imaginary friend that some children create. Other times it struck me that this was other than normal. Finally, I brought the phenomenon up with the psychiatrist who had been so supportive. When I explained it to her, she told me she was very comfortable that this was simply a coping technique and probably quite healthy. When I pressed her, needing some additional reassurance, she suggested bringing a second health professional in, a hypnotist. We did this, and both agreed that I M was simply a creative way of coping and I should not be concerned. But, I should be aware that if she went away I may react strongly. She was in effect, a support.

During the last few years that I lived with Dennis; IM remained that support. It wasn't until about five or six years after my divorce was finalized that she left. I scarcely noticed her absence, did not miss her, did not in fact, have any reaction to her exit. In a peculiar realization, that also affirmed my awareness that I had had no meaning for Dennis.

JOY, JUBILATION, AND A GLIMPSE OF HOPE

It would take several volumes to simply contain the joy filled feelings at the time of my daughter's birth. She was healthy, beautiful, perfect far beyond my expectations. There had never been and has never since been a more magnificent event in my life.

I looked forward to every doctor's appointment, was very careful with my diet, joined a neighbor who was also pregnant for a 2 ½ mile walk each day, got plenty of rest and let any tasks requiring lifting go. They simply had to wait, and it didn't bother me at all. One big thing missing was sharing all of this with the baby's father. I asked him to accompany me to the appointment where I would see the sonogram of the baby. He was too busy at work. I asked once or twice again but he never came. He did ask me a few times how I felt. I would respond with an honest statement, "good thanks, really good." Looking back, I remember one time when I was feeling especially lonely, I answered, "good generally. The pain has subsided." The same response, "oh, that's good." It was nasty of me as there had been no pain, but I felt validated that he was not listening to me and therefore forgave myself feeling justified. Still lonely, unsupported, sad but in a mean way, justified.

Narcissism

Jubilation and anxiety, joy and worry fought for dominance. At some point, when the fear was winning, I remember using a strange defense. I replaced the fear I had of another miscarriage or loss of the baby with the completely irrational fear of not recognizing labor. That fear I could deal with as I had never heard of any woman who had missed labor. I did not share this with anyone fearing how they would respond. It worked for me.

As my pregnancy progressed, I suggested that Dennis and I talk with the older children about what they might expect or feel about a new baby coming. "Oh, I already did that. They're fine." "But what did they say? They've mentioned to me that it might be fun and expressed some preferences for boy or girl." "But I thought we could talk to them together." "What is there to say? Like it or not, they'll learn to live with it." Another attempt at communication… Failed.

Parental Alienation, Triangulation, Narcissism,

Sometime after that, I was in the kitchen while my step daughter was in the living room reading. I heard her sigh, throw the book on the couch, run out to the kitchen and felt her punched me in the stomach saying, "you could get rid of that thing if you wanted to." I reached for her, tried to hug her and asked, "do you want me to get rid of it?" cringing at the word it. She turned, walked away and went up to her room. Fully aware that she had a big stake in this, having been the "baby" in the family for10 years and the only girl it certainly would have meaning for her. I waited a few minutes, went up to her room, brought her the book she had been reading and a snack. Sitting next to her on her bed I told her that I could understand that she had mixed feelings about this. She simply stated "no not really. I think it will be fun." I tried again, "oh I think it will be fun. But maybe not all fun. Babies take a lot of time, they are messy, inconsiderate, and sometimes very loud." "I don't want to talk about it." "That's fine, hon, but I think it would be good when you're ready." Despite one or two more efforts, she never would engage.

But that is not the focus of this work. Neither is the focus to whine, lay blame or make a list of complaints. It is rather to demonstrate and illustrate the serious behaviors that I missed.

Hopefully, this book will prevent others from falling into the same.

My daughter's delivery might be one of the easiest imaginable. My labor began around 2 to 3 in the morning and was rather gentle. I did wake Dennis to let him know and he did respond promptly sitting up on the side of the bed. I told him that I thought it would still be some time and if he preferred, he could go back to sleep. He did. I took a quick shower, a brief walk outside in the yard, and then realized that the contractions were coming much more closely. I went back and woke Dennis again. He got right up, dressed quickly and put my suitcase into the car. By then, it was time to leave.

On the way to the hospital, I did some of the classic antics but didn't care. On leaving the house I told Dennis to take his time and drive carefully thinking that we had no reason to rush because my labor pains were still far apart. Within three blocks or so I chastised him and insisted he go faster. On pulling into the emergency room, I panicked Because a black cat walked in front of the car; when registering, the receptionist, listed me as "an elderly prima gravida "Elderly!!?" (medical term for older than average first deliverer). I responded with an agitated "are you talking about me?" Then I was assigned to a room with a number that ended in 13. I would not go and insisted that I would not go to a room that was unlucky.

That all resolved, I was admitted and went to the labor room. My obstetrician was notified and arrived very quickly. He confirmed that labor was progressing normally and quickly, and he would be on hand for the delivery. On the way out of the room, he told the nurse that he would be down the hall "taking a nap." I was indignant. A nap?! When I was in labor?! How could he?! (More typical, irritable behaviors of women in labor.") I felt no pain, worked very hard but was supported by the joyful anticipation. Within just over an hour it was declared that I was in "transition". That was the signal to move from the labor room to the delivery room. Dennis was given a set of scrubs and he went into the bathroom to change. Moments later he came to me looking panicked. He said, "they have an automatic flush toilet. When I stood up, it flushed and now it looks like I wet my pants. What should I do?" My response was, "you're on your own Dennis. I'm busy right now." For a few years after that he did periodically chide me for being callous and unresponsive to his needs. That could have been an opportunity for joint amusement!

The birth happened so quickly and easily and when she was handed to Dennis, his first response was genuine tears, magnificent smiles and he said, "oh, a beautiful, perfect baby girl." I have never been so moved so jubilance, so grateful, so overwhelmed AND he was sharing it!

Some precious time with her and Dennis. I felt my own mild rage when the nurse came to take my little love to the new born nursery. As I was being wheeled to my room, I said to Dennis, "I am so thrilled. But unfortunately, I'm also hungry. Could you get me something to eat?". "I can't. I'll just about have time to get to Pennsylvania for the closing." "Dennis, just call them and tell them that our daughter was just born, and we need to change the date." "Change the date? Marie, I want that house this summer. It's important." "Vic, this is important to me. More important than anything else." "But if I don't go and sign the papers, it will delay the beginning of construction." "But if you do you, it will deprive me of sharing the greatest joy I've known." "She'll be around for a lot of years." And he put his coat on. I would not risk spoiling this day with one of his rages. He left the room. No kiss, no hug, no inquiry as to how I felt. The one thing he did do was grab a banana from the food trays being returned. When I first saw him coming back into the room I misunderstood and thought he was coming back to be with us. He handed me the banana and left.

d.t.: Zero Tolerance with no plan for caring for the families, AND no follow up,

Narcissism

I did refuse to allow that to interfere with or dilute my joy. But it also deprived us another opportunity to grow into a "we" and share a great joy.

When we brought my precious daughter home, he left almost immediately to drive his mother back to her home in Queens. On his way home, he totaled my car. So, when he came in, all his attention was focused on replacing the car. He did ask me a few times what new car I would want. I simply said it was not important to me today and it wasn't. And again, it was all about him

The next several months were filled with joy, love and everything wonderful about being with my new sweet daughter. I have a few memories of Dennis being affectionate with her and I cherish those memories. He would hold her, cuddle her and glow. I tried hard to see him anew. But I was so thrilled with my healthy, beautiful, loving daughter, that I was less aware of that than I might otherwise have been.

Narcissism, Physical Abuse

When she was about one and a half years old there was a funeral that I attended. It was on a Saturday morning, so I made sure that Dennis would be home. He assured me that he would. When I returned from the funeral, I was so happy to see her (it was the first time I had left her at all) that I spent some time hugging her and playing with her. Soon after that I decided to change her diaper and found a full handprint bruise on her buttocks!!. Now it was my turn to rage and I did. I brought her to him and said, "what is this?" His answer was that she was giving him a hard time getting dressed and he wanted to get to the bank. I stood directly in front of him, looked directly at him and said, "that is the last time this will happen." I gathered some clothes for her and for me and left the house. On the way out I said again firmly, maybe even menacingly, "THE LAST TIME." I stayed with her at my sister's home for two days and did not care how he or his children fared.

Between that event, the boa constrictor and my own overprotectiveness, it was the last time I left her alone for several years. Of course, it complied with my own wishes that I spend all my time with her. And of course, I reflected, examined and revisited the entire situation looking for failures on my part. Earlier, when she was only a few months old, I had heard on the radio that there was a home invasion and the perpetrator and thrown a baby across a room. I knew clearly that if that had been her, I would readily kill. I would not care about "excessive force, liability, alternative options". I was one ushered bees out of the house, walked around and hills, etc. I WOULD KILL! Now this was her father. No, I never had the temptation to kill. But I knew that she would never again be left alone with him.

There was never any conversation about that event except that at some opportunities I repeated, looking him directly in the eyes and saying firmly "THE LAST TIME". From that time on, my entire relationship with him became defensive, and not much else.

I relished every moment with her. I wanted it to go on forever. But, when she was about four years old, she said, "Mommy, I think I should go to school soon." My first reaction was to say, "school? You're going to stay right next to mommy until you're 35." We talked about school and decided to visit several of the preschools in the area. The first one we went to was right next door at the Bergen Humanist society. After a short time there, she turned to me and said very loudly, "it's too messy here, mommy, let's go home." Red faced, I took her home. We visited two or three other sites but when we got to the Montessori school in town, we both knew that this was where she belonged.

Silent Treatment

That evening I told Dennis that we had found a lovely preschool and both of us loved it. I asked if he would like to go and see it. His answer, "what's the point? It's clear that you and she have made the decision." He did not ask which school we had chosen, why we had chosen it, or where it was. That evening I went to the desk and wrote a check covering the first six months at the Montessori school. When he found that, the predictable rage occurred. "Marie, I've told you several times that I strongly believe in supporting the public school system. Maybe you don't understand, but the Montessori school is a private school. I will not pay for private school education." Aware that this time it was me who was unwilling to compromise, I again began chiding myself. But, in all honesty that ended rather quickly. Early the following morning I brought the check to the Montessori school and asked them to deposit it that same day. Yes, I was frightened. I was also wholly resolute. He ranted for days. I simply stayed out of the house as much as possible and ignored him. I did not disagree with him in principle about supporting the public school system. But over the past several years I had visited the elementary, middle and high schools many times. Although our town had the reputation for being the best integrated town in the country, there was no question that the high school had one door through which the black students entered, one through which the Hispanic students entered and one for white students. Unacceptable. On one visit to the middle school at the beginning of lunchtime I heard the teacher standing at the top of the stairwell yelling down, "Keep quiet. You're giving me a headache." Also, unacceptable. Sometime prior to that I had brought my daughter to a puppet show in the local private school. As we went into the school the students were also coming down to see the puppet show. On each landing, was a teacher saying something about going slowly, being careful of the people in front of and behind you and waiting to talk until you are at the bottom of the stairs. That was what I wanted my daughter to hear; be careful out of consideration and concern for others. So, while I agreed with the principle, this was my daughter's education, not a principle.

After a few weeks I revisited the topic. I asked Dennis if he wanted to visit the Montessori school. Our daughter would not be beginning for a few weeks when there would be an opening for her. He declined and repeated that it was not a school that he would pay for. The importance of the issue emboldened me, and I said, "Dennis, she's my daughter too. I have a say in which school she attends." "When you can pay, you get a say," he said. Further emboldened I responded, "No, I get a say." As soon as she began school, I began attending test marketing sessions, doing anything I could to earn some money. I used that for her schooling and supplemented it with checks from our account which I had only recently acquired signing privileges on. Unexpectedly, the only reaction from him was the silent treatment.

DT: the tweets came in torrents, some true; many completely untrue, unless he could find no way to tout his imagined successes. Then came the silence.

Narcissism

I, of course, was familiar with the word narcissism, BUT, had a minimal real comprehension of the full reality of that meaning. Just a few days before her high school graduation, Dennis was committed to a psychiatric unit nearby and began a series of electroshock therapy treatments. That was the same week that Amy had her final exams for her graduation. During one of her last exams, she became upset and was unable to complete the exam. She came home from school still very upset and told me what had happened. I drove to the school the following morning and requested a meeting with her homeroom teacher. That teacher explained to me that her grades for that exam would be failing. That meant her graduation would not happen. Horrified, I spoke with the teacher and explained that Amy's father had become ill and she was upset. On the other hand, she had been in the school for four years and was an exemplary student. I met a brick wall; she would not be permitted to graduate. I could not accept that, so I went to the principal's office. I was told that the principal had appointments for most of the day. I simply stated that I did not have anything more important to do and would be happy to wait. When I finally got to talk with her, I explained the situation, stated that our choice to have her in a Catholic school was based on the belief that values we held dear would be supported. She remained with her original position, that was school policy. I retorted that my daughter was more important than an arbitrary policy. After a few minutes, she relented and stated that Amy would have to retake the exam and pass it. That is just what happened, and she was assured of graduation.

Irrationally, I felt anger toward Dennis that he had "chosen" this precise time to be hospitalized and then was unable to support my efforts on her behalf.

She did graduate with her class and Eddy had picked up his father and driven him to the graduation. There certainly was no plan for a graduation party, but I did ask a few of my friends to come in support of her. During that party Dennis did take the opportunity to sneer at my friends, "I suppose you are all a pack of mackerel snappers (denigrating term for Catholics), too."

"He is not mean; he is not bad; his disordered world is all he has. He's doing his best; his best is not something I can detest ."

He had disparaged my cherished family, friends, my profession, my religion, all my personal qualities, everything that had meaning for me. He had even deprived me of hope. From the time I was a young teenager and had volunteered at a local nursing home, I had recognized the importance and value of hope. Those residents in the nursing home who had hope, be it to see their grandchildren graduate, have a sunny day, or find an appealing meal in front of them, but looked forward to something, thrived more successfully than those who were without hope. Now I really understood that and found myself among the hopeless.

My mantra no longer worked!

When I drove him back to the hospital later that day, he was silent, resentful, and even morose. Heading toward the parking lot he screamed, "don't park. I don't need you gloating over this. Just drop me at the front door."

After his discharge, things just became increasingly worse. He continually blamed me for his illness, his hospitalization, and his unhappiness. The afternoon after he came home, Eddy called to ask if he could borrow some money. The only part of the conversation I heard was "yeah, yeah, yeah, I'll send it today". He slammed the phone down and

Dennis went into a rage calling his son horrendous names, stating that he wanted to never see him again, and that the #$%^@#$ had never even asked how Dennis was, just asked for money

I had just begun working part time from home a few months before and was still not really earning a salary. But I did see hope that the agency was growing, and I counted on an income from that to continue financing her schooling. That soon came to fruition. I found it extremely offensive that he did not consider supporting the best school for her but only supporting his own principle. That continued through her private high school education. When it was time for her to go to college, she selected Scranton University. Dennis did not realize that this was a Jesuit private school and therefore wrote the check for the application and the first semester. I did not educate him about it. Soon there was some written communication from the school that he read and noticed on the letterhead that it said "Jesuit". Ranting, rages, silent treatment, etc. followed. I simply stayed out of the house as much as possible. At the end of the year and a half she changed and went to Ramapo College. I simply left him the bill and he paid it. There was no discussion whatsoever about why she had changed schools. From there, she went into AmeriCorps and then attended Bergen community college for a year. Because we were separated by the time, she went to Bergen Community College he agreed to fully pay for tuition. When she completed her year there, she was accepted at Columbia University. I sent a letter requesting that he pay at least half the cost with a copy of her acceptance letter to his lawyer to forward to him. I received a phone call a few days later from him screaming, "I do not pay for private education." I knew he was expressing his rage toward me, not her.

During that phone call he also screamed at me that I had destroyed our daughter. He went on to tell me that he had seen pictures of her at the government service program she had joined for a year. He claimed that it was obvious that she had been drinking and he had been told that she was doing a lot of that. That was very hard to hear. My guess is that there are many parents who worry about this especially when their children are away from home. I had also seen pictures of her with bottles of beer in her hand and her eyes looking glassy. Yet, I trusted her, thought that I knew her well enough and did not truly believe this. It was not a topic I wanted to discuss with her robe the phone and she would be home in a few months. I prayed and prayed that he was wrong. It was a cruel call to make.

No matter where I looked, with whom I spoke, nor the frequency or strength of my efforts, there was no improvement. One recollection I have is a day in the spring when for some reason, Dennis wanted to take a bureau down from the attic. We had drop-down stairs so, he went up and moved to the bureau to the top of the stairs. Laying it down on the side he tilted it into the stairwell. I was at the bottom expecting to guide it down to the bottom. However, the bureau became wedged in the opening to the stairs. Dennis pulled and pushed the bureau would not budge. It was too high for me to help. Dennis did suggest that I try to release it by going up two or three steps and pushing it up. I firmly declined; if I had succeeded the bureau would certainly have come down on top of me. I am horrified to remember my thoughts: "This could be the answer. Just leave him up there, go out. Stay away for a few days and that will end the misery." The thought in and of itself gave me such relief, such a feeling of emancipation, and finally a sense of hope. Of course, I went and found a neighbor to help. But the guilt still has not gone away.

I never hated Dennis. I feared him. But obviously there were no feelings of love between us and any hope I had felt earlier was gone. I did want freedom from the chaos and negative atmosphere we were living in. Reflecting on the awful thoughts I had when he was in the attic, I KNEW I had to find a way.

She received her acceptance to an Ivy League University on one day; and the very next day the bill came. Frankly, I thought that very tacky. At least give us some time to celebrate.

I don't remember the exact amount, but I do remember that it was over $57,000. I was in the midst of a divorce, did not know where I would land financially but knew that I would do it. The final cost was less than that because she did receive some scholarship money and her year in AmeriCorps contributed some as well. I again sent a message to his attorney requesting that he help her and again received a nasty phone call declining.

For sure, this was a way of retaliating against me without any concern for how it might affect his daughter. He was fully aware of my depleted financial resources and still wanted to hurt me. What an awful legacy to leave his daughter. Another example of the narcissistic, disordered thinking.

DT:: I will build a big beautiful wall (regardless of the cost to the American people in losing health care, opportunities, etc.) my management of the Puerto Rican disaster is an unsung success, I will release my tax returns…., Continuous and frequent implications that the American people are so dumb that they don't understand that MY image is more important than anything they might need or want. His conviction that he can guess I all the people in his base by lying, falsely accusing, viciously attacking, and generally deceiving them.

We lived in the same town with the northern campus of a large University. That university had a strong international program. It occurred to me that there might be international students needing to find housing. Luckily, I was correct, and they gave me a website on which to register. It was no time at all until I had students registered for housing for the whole second year of her schooling. That certainly helped.

I had stopped answering his phone calls by that time but listened to his message that he would be stopping ALL financial support as I now had a source of my own income.

So! he was pumping his children for information about me. My first response was to be almost pleased that he still had that much interest in me. Happily, I very quickly became aware that this was not interest, but rather in need to renew his primary scapegoat. There seemed to be no end to his rage and anger. I stopped checking his messages then.

There are many books for those dealing with someone who has narcissistic personality disorder and realizes it. Every last one of them that I have read advises that if you are preparing to terminate the relationship the predominant principle is NO CONTACT. I learned then that that was the only effective and more healthy manner in which to free yourself from the very destructive interactions in those relationships.

It was during the third month of her third year at college that I received a phone call from her. She simply said, "Mom, I'm at the hospital. Dad just died." A plethora of emotions descended.

I so badly wanted to hug/help her, but the boundaries had been drawn by her (no discussion about her father) and, while I disagreed with her about that, feeling that communication would be preferable even if painful, I accepted that she needed them. All I could say was, "I'm sorry Jen, truly sorry", and "I love you." I felt so inadequate, helpless and impotent. She was not entirely alone. She had her three half siblings to share her grief. But I am her mother, I love her fiercely, and I am absent.

As for the time of separation, she would meet her father about once a week for dinner. Every time she came back, her mood was one of great anger. She would slam doors, stomp up the stairs, and avoid all conversation. It saddened me greatly. So, without referring to the dark moods, I simply suggested that she drive to meet him wherever they were having dinner, set the boundaries for conversation and if she was uncomfortable, she could just leave and drive home. She did follow that suggestion but never commented on it and would never discuss it.

That was about eighteen years ago, November, 2000 and only after his death and burial have I come to recognize, understand, and appreciate the significance of this. For sure, that is one of the things I will never forgive myself for. Because I held nothing like his hatred within me, it never occurred to me to do anything that would alienate his three children from him. Never! To begin with, they were of course, his children and not mine clearly. But that was simply not an area I would have considered. It did not even occur to me that the children should be put in the position of having to choose. In terms of our daughter, I cannot recall saying anything negative to her about her father. Then, one day when she was going to meet him for dinner. I asked her to bring a plastic bag full of his mail to him. She got angrier than I had ever seen her before. With a level of fury, she said, "no, that's between you and him. Leave me out of it." At the time, her reaction seemed extreme. But, of course, we were all under stress at the time. With the benefit of hindsight, I now understand that she was being seduced (gaslighted) into the acceptance of her father's disordered perception of me. I did not know precisely what that meant as well as I should have, and, in fact, did not truly appreciate the stress that that placed on her. My love for her was so total, simple, and unconditional that it simply did not cross my mind that that time for her must have been very nearly intolerable. That may indeed be what I regret more than anything. I was not at all there for her; I ought to have pushed a little harder to maintain communication with her; I ought to have been far wiser about the dynamics of NPD. From that time, until about three years ago, I trusted that the whole of our relationship would improve beyond the monosyllabic conversations we mostly had. 🚩

I was seriously wrong. Culpably wrong.

Triangulation, Victimization

I was so seriously wrong about that and it will forever be intolerably painful for as long as I live. I deeply love her, like her, admire her, and with every day wish to share her and her beautiful family. That may indeed be the strongest motivation for the writing of this book. He had projected such a hateful picture of me that she was now left with a rage and hurt that very likely may harm her and there was nothing I could do about it. She had incorporated the disordered image of me that her father had foisted upon her and his biological children. And I now had no power to help her get to know the real person who was her mother. Nor, would she ever know my family of origin which was such a rich and wonderful one. I do, however, have a lasting joy that I played a significant role in bringing this wonderful young woman to our world. In addition, and maybe even greater joy, is knowing that she and her wonderful husband have a lovely life with their three children who are beyond any hopes I may ever have had.

I did not revel in the death of my ex-husband at all even though it had been a contentious, painful relationship. I am still unable to call it a marriage and think of it as a "non-marriage". Neither did I feel a sense of grief **or** loss. Instead, a profound sorrow, which I did not fully understand, descended and swallowed me. The sorrow was certainly for my daughter but, in time, it became clear that it was as much for her father's life. He was a bright, hard-working, sincere, charming person who opposed violence, littering, cruelty to animals and was firmly committed to his children and supporting local business. He led a thoughtful, ethical life and yet was so unhappy, so lonely.

The rare times we talked about our earlier lives he could recall no names of childhood friends, army buddies, college friends nor did he have any that I was aware of during his adult life. His relationships with his mother and brother were tenuous, and even contentious. At the time, I rationalized that, recognizing that he had had a mentally ill first wife, three children a demanding job and a good-sized home to maintain, he certainly had little time for a personal/social life. It took me long, much too long, to realize why he was so friendless. In that context I was also realizing that he and his children had a fiercely loyal relationship but not one that was affectionate at all. Except for his younger son, I never saw any affection among the four of them. He was clearly committed to them, did all the right things like attending school events, sporting events, checking on this school progress and buying them whatever they needed. But, affection or enjoyment of their company was not at all evident.

She was not entirely alone. She had her three half siblings to share her grief. But I am her mother, I love her fiercely and I am absent.

That was almost eighteen years ago, November 30, 2002 and only now have I begun to understand. I am still unable to call it a marriage. Neither did I feel a sense of grief or loss. Instead, a profound sorrow, which I didn't fully understand, descended and swallowed me. The sorrow was certainly for my daughter. But, in time, it became clear that it was as much for her father's life. He was a bright, hardworking, sincere, charming person who opposed violence and littering, cared about animals, tried to support entrepreneurship and was committed to his children and supporting local business. He led a thoughtful, ethical life and yet was so enraged, so unhappy, so lonely. He had his family who definitely cared about him but there was such an inability to make any affective or even real intellectual connection with them. I learned over time that this had been true throughout most of his life.

The rare times we talked about his earlier life, he could recall no names of childhood friends, army buddies, college friends, nor did he have any that I was aware of during his adult life. His relationship with his mother and brother was tenuous and even contentious. At that time, I rationalized that since he had had a mentally ill first wife, three children, a demanding job and a large home to maintain. He had little time for a personal/social life.

About two years after my husband retired, I came home after work and found him, not surprisingly, in his recliner reading. I called to him from the door, "Hi! How was your day?"

Next to him on the floor I noticed our colander. He looked up at me with nothing short of hate in his face and growled "why the f--- do we have a red colander"? I hardly recognized this person as the man I had married. It was terrifying to see that level of hate. He had fought a lifelong battle with depression and had valiantly fought that good fight. I feared he was losing it.

Since his retirement, it had become evident that the depression had begun to gain control. As I looked at him, I wavered between fear and painfully deep sorrow. I thought to explain that the red colander had been in the house from the time before I married him. However, it took only seconds to realize that he was no longer reachable. Over our 21 years of marriage I had learned the warning signs. I had also developed a safety strategy for responding. I left the house and headed back to my office, a place of refuge, being careful to lock the doors behind me. For about six years I had kept a change of clothes and a small amount of cash in the trunk of my car and had used them for such events several times. During one of those years I had slept on the floor of my office dozens of times and the frequency escalated as the years went on. I had had Dennis arrested five times for assault and never wanted to do that to him again. Looking back, the caretaker in me did not consider that I did not want to do that to him but did not consider the consequences to myself.

"Wow, I'm four for four! Why can't I get a break? My mother, Mary Ann, Joan, and now you. Not one of you ever gave a damn."

I had been working at the dining room table. He was in the next room, the living room. I knew he had been drinking again but this sounded like he was in greater pain. I walked in and asked, "What can I do, Dennis?" but was shocked to see tears pouring down his face. He was weeping copiously. He looked old, tired and desperate.

He did not look at me but said twice "I am so lonely, so alone. Why?" It was heartbreaking, and I moved toward him intending to sit near him and hug him. Instead, he picked up the book on his lap, threw it at me and said "Don't pretend. It's too late." As desperately painful as the whole scene was, the Pollyanna in me had the thought that maybe he was ready to develop some insight, maybe this could be a turning point for him.

Going to the love seat across from him, I sat and said "of course it's not too late, Dennis. I really do care about you and have. But I don't know how to help you. Have you talked with Dr. Milano about how much you're hurting?"

 "I don't want a doctor, I want a family and a wife, even a friend." No amount of reassurance seemed to console him. Then he looked up angrily at me and said, "you're enjoying this, aren't you?" When I saw the hate in his eyes, I understood that he was not ready to accept any rational or caring response. So, I just sat across from him quietly. Eventually he fell asleep. Then it was my turn to cry. He was the most alone person I had ever known by far.

During most of the time we had been married he did a very moderate amount of drinking but since his retirement he would drink most of the afternoon and evening. I couldn't reach him. I was certain that he wanted someone to reach him but not at all certain that it could be me. He had created within him due to his need to project any possible or perceived imperfections within himself on to me. In his perception I was very definitely a focus for his rage and hate. He had a rage within him that prevented him from accepting any sign of affection or caring. I decided to wait until his next appointment with his psychiatrist and ask if I could accompany him.

Parental Alienation, Narcissism, Gaslighting

They were two Easter Sundays, the first when my daughter was two and the second two years later when the plans were to go to his mother's home for Easter dinner. On the first, Dennis had said we would leave the house at noon. My daughter, as usual, resisted getting dressed and I was not especially firm with her. When I got her into her pretty new Easter dress she wanted to dance and it, play in it and show it off. By the time we came downstairs at about 12:15, no one was home. At first, I assumed that they had gone to fill the car with gas and would return shortly. They never did I spent the day walking around a neighboring town trying to quell the hurt. I was so hurt I didn't even have a name for it. When we all came back home that evening, I asked Dennis why he had left, and his response was simply, "We said noon. When we say at noon, believe it." When began to explain he simply walked away and went upstairs. On the second occasion, I was ready, but they had already left. By then, I knew better than to challenge him.

Not only was I hurt, but the message to the three older children was very clear, as it was to me, and I was sure it was clear to them. Marie is not a family member. The four of us of the family. How destructive! By then I had learned that any attempt to negotiate with him or express my fears and concerns would be futile. In fact, they would lead to more rages and rants. Now I had to decide if I could live with that. The role of nanny was not one I had sought, nor one I anticipated with any pleasure. But the major issue of another female abandoning the children dominated my thoughts, feelings, and unfortunately, my decision.

In 1982, I had applied for and received a license to operate an adoption agency in New Jersey. Initially, the only service we offered was pre-adoption homestudy evaluations for families who were adopting from foreign countries and post-placement supervision reports. This enabled me to work only part-time one or two evenings a week; it also gave me contact with some normalcy which I desperately needed. But after about five years the agency had begun adoptive placement programs in Romania, China, Colombia, South America and El Salvador. As each program began, I did travel to those countries to sign agreements with the government, hire and train staff and prepare for families to travel there. As each program opened, I would inform Dennis and give him some information about that particular program. Several years later I heard him talking to a neighbor and saying, "yes, yes! She's still working, and I think she has two or three programs in South America." He had not even heard or retained just about anything I had said to him. Because I had a free companion ticket American Express, I had asked him a couple of times if he wanted to travel with me. The response was consistent and simple, "no, not me." He never did. Neither did he ever show the slightest interest in what I was doing nor did he offer to drive me to or from the airport, etc.

I was enormously grateful that this opportunity had presented itself. It was of course hard, time-consuming work, especially because I was new to it, especially new to the business to dimension, which I had never been involved with. But it was almost 100% positive, rewarding, and more than gratifying. So desperately did I need that. As a licensed, psychiatric social worker I could have found work with multi-problem families, disturbed psychiatric patients, drug addicts, etc. I would never have been able to summon the energy or potency needed to work in problem areas. In addition, I was seeing that I was capable, smart, and able to work well with people from all different cultures.

While the progress, growth and success of the agency was enormously rewarding, mainly it provided me an arena in which my normalcy was obvious even to me. That enabled me to move emotionally away from the self-recrimination, self-doubt, pervasive self-examination about my part in the failed marriage. At no point, and even until today, did I feel completely free of responsibility for its failure. But I was then and am now 100% certain that I did everything that I could. Sometimes, hindsight gives you perspective and the ability to see what you missed at the moment. That has not happened. I truly believe that the level of Dennis's illness and the particular characteristics of it, would have led to the failure no matter what I did. And there was evidence that this was true. He had no friendships, no enduring satisfactory family relationships and no enduring relationships with colleagues, neighbors, friends.

Could I abandon him to that lonely, empty existence? On the other hand, could I and should I remain in it being totally incapable of finding a way to improve it?

On my way home from one of my foreign trips, in the solitude and quiet that the night flight offered me, I made a simple resolution. The next time I felt threatened or was physically abused, would be the last time.

It only took four days. I had been out one evening doing errands and when I came home the house was dark. I felt relieved assuming that Dennis had gone to sleep. But when I walked in the front door, he leapt up from the dining room chair in the far corner of the room. He had the largest of our corning ware dishes in his hand and started screaming that that was the last time I could meet with my boyfriend. He threw the dish at me, hit me in the shin, caused a large cut and I left the house. I went directly to the police precinct, filed complaint, and drove back, parking near the house but not going in. The police arrived very shortly, and I saw them removing him from the house in handcuffs. I felt no guilt, no remorse and did no second-guessing of my decision. Gigantic sadness engulfed me, but I went into the house feeling safe for the first time in years.

It may have been a kind of callousness; it may have been just the relief; it may have been a conviction that what I had done was the right thing. In any case, I never gave second thoughts nor had I any regrets about the decision.

At the time I had him arrested I had also applied for an order of protection. I went before the judge the next morning and obtained a copy. For about 3 to 4 days, I simply felt relief from the fear. I assumed that he had gone to stay with his son, Brian and Brian and had bailed him out. But it was a couple of weeks until I even concerned myself with that. During those weeks, I simply enjoyed the freedom to be in my home without fear.

At some point over the next few weeks I learned that he had rented an apartment in a town nearby. I had no curiosity about exactly where. I was aware that my telephone rang several times during the night. The first time I answered the phone the rage came through immediately and I was unwilling to listen to more of it then. I noted the telephone number and stopped answering calls from that number. From then forward I turn the ringer off and did not answer calls from that number if caller ID informed me that it was Dennis calling. So, each night at about 9 PM I would turn the ringer off. He called my office a number of times, but I always made excuses for not taking his calls. Again, it was extremely awkward, and I had

had enough practice lying to him that I simply made up reasons why I was not accepting his calls. The entire time since his last arrest I gave very little thought to him. I simply prayed for a return to normalcy for me and something good to happen for him. It was the most peace filled time I had known in years and I simply absorbed it, even wallowed in it. It was several weeks later when he came to the door requesting entry. I would not even open the door. He got angry, and yelled threats and persisted for what seemed a long time but was probably only 15 to 20 minutes. Later that day, I called the locksmith and had the locks changed. "Now, I can begin to be at home." Unfortunately, that was only a wish. For as long as I continued to live there, the memories remained, and it remained "his" home. It was located in an area where I had a strong support group and that was important. It was also my daughter's childhood home and I felt that might be important too.

Within a few days he came back to the house with his oldest son. He actually tried his key in the lock. More rage. That only served to reinforce my conviction that I had done the right thing. The following morning, I got a call from the local police station that he had requested that they accompany him into the house to obtain some belongings. I agreed that that would be fine. The policeman advised me to stay within viewing distance so that I could monitor what he took; but to stay at a distance so as not to be a provocative factor. I did just that. Now I felt the sadness return. This had been the home he had purchased, raised his children in, and expected to retire in. He looked suddenly much older, tired and furious. He went to the bedroom, library, basement and living room collecting the things he wanted to bring. There was nothing I objected to and he was ready to leave. He looked over at me as he was on his way out and said, "now I'll really never forgive you. The only two decent things you did in 20 years was put up graduation pictures of the kids and suggest a closet under the stairs in the Pocono house." Yes, it was painfully sad but the hate in his face again confirmed that this was the only choice. I had cared for and provided for his three children, becoming Ann Marie's brownie leader, making her graduation dress because we could not find one in her size when she was graduating from elementary school; I had painted or papered all but two rooms in the house, I had supported all of the efforts he had expressed to be an active member of the Humanist society, I had done my very best to be careful with money, especially early on when he was recovering from his expensive divorce, I had learned a lot about caring for the property and enjoyed that. So, within a short time, I was the one who trimmed hedges, planted groundcover, maintained the garden, etc. I never did mow the lawn as the property was in the three tiers on a fairly steep slope and there were two healthy men in the family. I always sought to make his life easier because that is of my very nature. I learned a lot from him about healthful eating and tried very hard to accommodate his wishes. I attended social events at both the NYSE and BECS, etc. but no matter what effort I made, there was always criticism.

Yes, I still continually went through self-recrimination, self-criticism, exploring ways I could "do better." There seemed no end to that. If only I had accepted that it would not have made a difference, there was so much more I could have accomplished. HE WAS UNHAPPY, it was not my shortcomings or those of his colleagues, or neighbors, or…or…, etc. No matter how I had tried he would still have been a terribly unhappy person. I was aware of some shortcomings I had, but now the list continually grew. AND, there was no confirmation that it was accurate. INTERNAL CHAOS AND CONFUSION REIGNED!

I remembered several times when I had prepared Friday dinner; he came home from work and the children came downstairs with their suitcase and they left for skiing in the Poconos. I stopped making dinner on Fridays, but was fearful of asking for a discussion and the problem went unsolved.

An actual civil divorce was something very far from my mind. We had been divorced for so many years by now that a formal divorce seemed anti-climactic. For a good year or two, I simply tried to heal, enjoy the peace and some of my friendships. There were certain sights and sounds that provoked the same feelings of fear I had known for so long. But that was much more manageable than the way I had been living.

At one point in time I had to travel for work. I prepared for the trip, informed neighbors who would keep an eye on the house and was ready to leave. At the last minute, it occurred to me that

Dennis might have heard that I was going away through the children or somehow. I call the police station, informed them of my plans and asked them to be extra vigilant. Just before I left panic struck me. I took a large bag of flour, poured some on the floor inside the kitchen door and some in front of the window in the back of the house. When I returned, I saw the footprints and flour, called the police and had them witness the scene. They offered the possibility of filing charges of breaking and entering and/or violating the order of protection. They were extremely respectful informing me of my options and what they would mean but exerting no pressure. They measured the footprint and confirmed that it was a size eleven; the size shoe that Dennis wore. Over the next few days I noticed that some things were missing. I didn't care. I simply heightened my vigilance.

During the next few months, the late-night phone calls persisted (I noted that from the caller ID feature), there were a couple of calls during the day and on weekends. Other than that, there was no contact with me. He did, about once a week, take our daughter to dinner. Every time she came back there would be slamming doors, the angry look on her face and it was obvious she was upset. But she was adamant that there would be no discussion around her father. I did make the suggestion that she make arrangements to meet him at a restaurant and drive there. She could tell her father that she did not want to discuss me with him either and if he did, she could leave and drive home. I believe she did that twice.

Eventually, I received divorce papers through registered mail. I signed them and returned them within a day or two. I retained an attorney and also sent a letter to my attorney with a copy for his. I am a certified divorce mediator and suggested that we consider using a mediator as neither was contesting the divorce. It was several weeks before I received a letter from his attorney declining the suggestion. I had expected that. I was fully aware from very early on that I would be in a stronger position if I filed divorce. Dennis had admitted to assaulting me on five separate occasions, had already been divorced once, could have found almost no one who would have testified on his behalf and constantly betrayed his own mental ill health with his frequent distortions of truth and reality, contradictions and protestations about his all victimization. I had no inclination to hurt him still. Yet, it was remarkable to see how little he actually knew about me in writing. In the complaint for divorce he listed both of my parents' first names incorrectly, he did not know what college or graduate school I had completed and gave a number of incorrect facts about my background. He could still hurt me. How little involvement he had had in my life! I think that was the first time that I had a mental picture of him covered in shrink wrap. He was incredibly isolated from any real involvement with anyone I knew of. It was one of the saddest moments of my life. And I had to face how and why I continued to care about him.

"He is not mean; he is not bad; his disordered world is all he has. He's doing his best; his best is not something I can detest."

Within days of receiving that letter I received a letter from my attorney explaining that she was moving out of state and therefore would be unable to represent me. I found the second attorney and had my first meeting with him. He said, "okay, tell me the six worst things he ever did to you." "No, I said I don't want to destroy him I just want to live separately from him." "Your choice."

For the second and third meetings I sat waiting about 45 minutes each time. His office window overlooked a large parking lot on the far side of in which was a motel. Both times I watched him walk out of the motel with his secretary. After it happened the second time, I informed him that his services were no longer needed. I found a third attorney, and notified Dennis's attorney, there were four or five messages on my home phone from Dennis saying things like, "you see you are a bitch. Even lawyers can't stand you." In another message he said, "if you make any attempt to communicate with my kids, you will pay for it." It didn't really matter; he had caused so much parental alienation already and they were fully adults. I never understood his need to pass on his negative feelings toward me to his children. It was nothing more than revenge and receptacles for his disordered perception of me and there was so much of him that would have been a far better legacy. Maybe I also ordered to have reported his violations of the order of protection to the police, but I wanted less and less involvement in his illness. At this point, I just wanted it done. All I really felt toward him was tremendous sadness; the rage in his voice, the knowledge that he was just about friendless, the fear that he was hopeless and the awareness that he had little else in his life but rage. No matter how burdensome the sadness was, I felt fully certain FOR THE FIRST TIME IN YEARS that this was the correct course of action.

Parental Alienation Triangulation

During the divorce negotiations, he contested everything. That was not a surprise. The one issue that held the divorce up for almost two years was that he insisted that I owned the adoption agency that I had founded. The agency was a not for profit corporation and therefore not owned by me or anyone else. We had two accountants, a corporate lawyer, and printed matter describing the basics about management of a not-for-profit corporation. He would not accept any of them. Finally, my lawyer suggested that he was certainly smart enough to understand but was using that as a means of not paying the property taxes, mortgage or any other bills for me and our daughter. He suggested having a subpoena sent to him requiring that he appear before a judge, be ordered to pay those bills and move toward finalization. I agreed.

Once he received the subpoena his rage seemed to escalate. He would very often, on his way home from the gym in the late morning, park his car one or two blocks from the house and remain there as long as my car was in the driveway. His late-night calls continued but were of little concern as by now I had a cell phone, he did not have that number and I turned the landline off in the late evenings. The last message I heard was that our daughter who was away at a government program, was clearly becoming "a drunk". He had seen photos of her, and she was clearly a "big time drinker". I soon stopped listening to any messages he left. It had become clear that it was necessary to do that and wise for me to completely refrain from any contact whatsoever. Within two or three weeks of this realization it became easier. I certainly felt some sadness for him but absolutely no guilt. That felt good!

A short time before the subpoena was delivered, I received a call from my stepdaughter, Ann Marie. She explained that she and her husband had run into some unexpected financial problems. They were close to losing their house but did have one offer which was below what they had hoped. Her father suggested they ask if they could stay with me for a time months; her father was buying a house and they could move in with him when that was accomplished. She said it might be as much as 2 to 3 months. Of course, I agreed. They closed on the sale, put most of the furniture in storage; I moved out of my bedroom which was next to a room they could use for their daughter and, largely due to Ann Marie's organizational skills, the move was accomplished with very little disruption. About a week or two after they moved in, Ann Marie asked if I would mind taking care of their daughter in the evenings for a few hours. She explained that her husband, who was not working at the time, got very tired caring for her all day and when she, Ann Marie, came home from teaching she was also very tired. In addition, the stress of the sale of the house and the move left them needing some time alone together. My first inclination was to say," Certainly", wanting to be as much help to them as possible. But I guess I had finally begun to learn. My response was, "I would love to help, Ann Marie. And will when I can. But, remember that I'm working full-time too and often have meetings in the evenings. If there are some days when I can help, I would love it and am more than willing." I was happy to note the growth in myself; she certainly had an expression of resentment but, I didn't care.

I continued to go about my life as I would and on some occasions, I did babysit and enjoyed it. Their daughter was about a year old, delightful, and sheer pleasure to have in the home. It certainly was a joy to experience the complete simplicity of a child. They were with me for about 11 months, I think. I did not disrupt the life I had begun to develop and was enjoying both, my new, burgeoning, normal life and the presence of their family. Once they moved, I never heard from them again.

Soon after they moved, the divorce was finalized in a very anticlimactic, nondramatic hearing in court. I had expected to feel a sense of liberation, relief, freedom. I didn't. When I saw Dennis in court, he looked old, angry and sad. I got no pleasure from that at all. But I also was very clear that this was the very best alternative and had a certain sense of peace. Yes, I felt sad too, but mainly peaceful and that was so nourishing.

A few days later, as I was driving home, I passed a local liquor store and saw him coming out. I have always felt sad that that was my last glimpse of him alive.

Proxy Recruitment, Gaslighting, Parental Alienation

It was a lot later and over several years, that it became clear that he had begun to gaslight them. All of them were very intelligent people. It was unintelligible to me that if the reality was that I was all the terrible kinds of things he assigned to me, why would he suggest that his daughter and her family moved in with me for almost a year? It also made me realize the strength of gaslighting and the enormous disassociation he had from reality. Then again, the question was there: why did they allow themselves to be so deceived by gaslighting when we had just lived together all that time and they saw nothing of the qualities that he had assigned to me?

This realization further clarified the destructiveness of NPD. I was horrified.

To take away the support his children and grandchildren would've had from me and had had from me, to deprive them of the ability to share memories, to continually learn more about their family of origin, etc. so deliberately and so thoroughly, horrified me. On the other hand, they were all adults, smart adults, and had made their own choices. Yes, I had begun to really appreciate the power of gaslighting, but I had not seen that it would go this far and hurt all of them so badly.

The mantra," *"He is not mean, he is not bad; his disordered world is all he has. He's doing his best; his best is not something I can detest."* was no longer meaningful. And I saw it as exceedingly naïve! Perhaps he was not deliberately mean, but his behaviors were beyond that, reprehensible, and so very destructive. What a legacy to leave for your children! Misguided hate? No, serious NARCISSISTIC PERSONALITY DISORDER!!! The damage had already been done and his children and I had, and still are, paying a very heavy price.

A few years after his death, I was going to a meeting with a neighbor and was navigating. I suggested we make a left turn and immediately realized that the turn was not where I had suggested but one light farther. The panic that struck me was so disproportionate to the error I had made that I could not avoid the realization that I was damaged, badly damaged. On that same trip my companion had asked if I would mind stopping at his son's house for a few moments to pick something up. His son, now a full adult, had been a friend of my stepsons all through elementary school. While I chatted for a few moments with his son in law I learned that when he and other friends had come to our home to play after school, they were always on alert for Dennis's arrival home from work. I joked with him that no matter how many times I invited them to stay for supper, they never did. His response was stunning. "Oh no Marie! We always got out of there to avoid him. He was mean! He scared us".

For the first time in my life, I was unable to forgive, a quality I believed strongly in but had to relinquish or at least we develop and grow in. This harm was intolerable to me and there was no opportunity to resolve it. Still and again I was having to relinquish my own values and personal commitments for the sake of his NPD!!! Prayer? Therapy? Support and friendships? From whom? He had deprived me of the children I loved, and my support system, friendships, and just about every other option.

I was aware at some point that Dennis and his son, Eddy, had gone to the house in the Poconos for a weekend. They had been taking down a tree and the trunk or a large limb fell on Dennis's leg. Apparently, he had serious fractures and had to be medevacked to a hospital. I did have the impulse to offer to make some meals and bring them to him. But my better judgment stepped in and I resisted that. Soon after that I learned that he had cancer. At first it did not seem to be extremely serious, he had cancer of the fatty tissue and there was an available surgery that held promise. He went into the hospital in New York City, had the surgery which was apparently successful. However, within a short time he died from an infection resulting from the surgery.

Triangulation, Parental Alienation, Scapegoating, Gaslighting

During the time that he was seriously ill, his anger led him to tell his children that if he were to die, I was to be prohibited from going to the wake or funeral. Again, I was fully aware that he had passed on his distorted perception of me to his children, drawn them into his hate and given no thought at all to the fact that he was depriving his children of an additional source of support and shared memories.

There was also a cruel irony in the fact that he had died of a type of cancer that likely came from ingesting cancer-causing material. It was terribly sad as he mocked me continually for my poor eating habits. I did attend the wake, at an off time and with the permission of the funeral parlor as I felt free now of his controlling behaviors and truly felt I wanted to say a last goodbye. I'm happy that I did that.

SECTION TWO

<u>ARE YOU A PROBABLE TARGET?</u>

Are you currently or potentially a "target" for someone within the NPD spectrum? It's a really important question everyone should have an opportunity to examine. I have talked with therapists, read extensively, joined blogs, and gleaned what I truly believe will be helpful, clear, and informative information and guidelines.

Many of the books I have read were helpful, but many portray a very cynical outlook about NPD. And I believe this perspective derives from the conviction that the harmful dynamics of an NPD afflicted person are deliberate, conscious, and intended to be hurtful. Now, and too late, I realize that that was naïve, wishful thinking. Were that the case then maybe several methods of treatment would be helpful. On the contrary, those dynamics are developed based on the very deep but unconscious needs of the person. In addition to their lack of awareness about the hurtful dynamics, the need to retain their harmful defenses are severe and not conscious. One book I read written by a self-proclaimed NPD person talked about how he went about deliberately targeting and finding a suitable mate in a very conscious way. I don't know that that occurs with most, as no one with NPD seems to be able or willing to develop that much self-awareness. Or, that person was much more conscious of their dynamics than the average.

In all of my research the dynamic which was most quickly obvious was scapegoating. In fact, a short time after my divorce, I met a very kind, intelligent, good man. On our second or third date, we began to talk about living alone. His first remark was, "It is hard. You have no one to blame anything on." That was our last date. I felt nothing short of panic.

Most of the characteristics that might make you vulnerable to a person with NPD are very common and in other contexts very positive. I am merely suggesting that both reflecting on your own personality and the reactions and reflections of others close to you is a wise thing. I am not suggesting that any changes be sought, but rather that a wise, educated, balanced, and somewhat accurate awareness of your SELF be sharply in focus.

 A "CARETAKER_The most common trait which will attract an NPD afflicted person are those of the "caretaking" personality. If you are someone who enjoys making the lives of others easier and more pleasant, you should be very aware of that; enjoy that as a trait and go about doing just that. But, in developing relationships, have an awareness that the meaning of caretaking may make you more attractive to someone with NPD. They will be aware that your instinct will be to protect them, not exploit or broadcast any failings you may see. And, importantly, be certain that you have also developed a sharp awareness of the need to take care of yourself as well.

B   TRUSTING   Because their disordered worlds cause their responses to be erratic, unpredictable, and they NEED someone to be trusting whenever their behaviors become unpredictable or unreliable.

C. Attractive and intelligent to support their continuous NEED for narcissistic supplies to project an image of someone who is a high achiever, above average, and heading for what they see as "great achievements".

D. Forgiving as they have learned that they can be self-involved, erratic and impulsive. They have learned to seek out relationships with people who easily forgive.

E. Lacking in very high self-esteem and confidence this will allow for them to manipulate, gaslight and bully their partner.

F. Independent allowing them to isolate and alienate you depriving you of support and accurate reflection on the relationship. It will also allow them to pursue their interests, desires and plans without you depending on their interest, support or even input.

G. Pleaser affording opportunities to obtain support and encouragement for their own interests, projects, desires without objection. Most often someone who enjoys and derives their own gratification from pleasing others will focus on that rather than seeking the same from their partner

H. Non-ambitious in this situation, the NPD person can be fully absorbed in pursuing their own path knowing that their partner will be satisfied to do the more mundane parts of their lives.

REFLECTIONS, LEARNING AND CLARIFYING

The scenarios in this book will be seen as very negative and perhaps, self-pitying, even whining. But, the purpose and essence of this project is to provide insight into the symptoms of NPD and hopefully prevent others from being harmed by it as I was. Many of the symptoms and behaviors are subtle and even similar to the behaviors of many people. It is the <u>extent</u> to which they are imposed, the severity of them, the relative harm they are doing and, to some extent the tolerance of the person relating to them. It was so late when I realized how destructive those symptoms were to me. But worse, it took so very long for the awareness in me to realize that my comfort, my safety, my wishes were important too. I believe that one of the most common and significant attributes of the target for an NPD is those who demonstrate the characteristics known as "caretaker". That is certainly true of me. I was rarely happier than when I was able to make someone else more comfortable, happy, and in general better off. There have been times when I thought of this characteristic as being somewhat arrogant. However, throughout my young life, I had come to enjoy that dimension in myself as well as in others. It may be what some would see as arrogance, but it may also be an attitude of giving and caring/loving. It has never become something I have regretted, felt any shame in, or tried to abolish.

Once again, it is important to remember that self-care is crucial and for that reason everyone has some level of narcissism. That is healthy. And once again I want to state that the extreme divisiveness, destruction and hurt are most often not the result of narcissism; but rather the dynamics of someone who has a severe personality disorder as well as an overdose of narcissism.

Hopefully, obtaining the vocabulary to describe the personality disorder will allow some to develop the ability to recognize it, use the vocabulary provided herein to define it, and thereby be able to make wise and healthy decisions for themselves.

If you are a person who has been involved with someone who has NPD for any significant amount of time, be well aware that in addition to all of the above forms of abuse, you have, in addition probably been deprived of all the benefits of feeling loved and appreciated. This is very important; your self-esteem and sense of self-worth have not only been deprived of nutrition but have systematically been denigrated and destroyed. Find help to rebuild the wonderful person you could become.

A SERIOUS MATTER TO GIVE SERIOUS CONTEMPLATION TO

Scapegoating, gaslighting and parental alienation are three extremely common behaviors of those who have narcissistic personality disorder. All are destructive, divisive and ones we should all be on alert for.

Scapegoating will mostly harm a partner.

Gaslighting and parental alienation will harm the children of any affected relationships and very seriously so.

Any person who has a serious level of NPD, **WILL** defend themselves very strenuously against taking responsibility for any failures. Or, any threat that they may be seen as responsible for them. This very definitely and primarily includes a parent. Consider and learn as much as possible, obtain as much support, emotional help, guidance as you can because the consequences of remaining ignorant about this can so seriously damaged children as well as yourself.

At the same time, keep in mind that one with NPD will most probably value loyalty over loving or caring. The loyalty provides them with some security but also with ongoing narcissistic supplies which they need desperately.

If there are children who are part of the relationship, and there is the threat of the relationship ending, or even just a perceived threat or fear, the partner with NPD very well may begin to gaslight the children. The children will absorb some of the information because they well may perceive the self-projected image of the affected parent victimizing themselves and will naturally tend to try to support that parent. That is actually a kind and loving response to a suffering parent. However, in one with NPD it will most likely lead to parental alienation as the NPD parent NEEDS the narcissistic supplies provided by the loyalty of their children.

<u>NO child should EVER be put in the position of having to choose between their parents.</u> There is no objective reason_for them to do so and the results might be devastating.

If you are aware of any implications that this is happening, ACT!

The better understanding you have, the more you will be able to explain to your children what is happening and help them defend against it. If you choose to do that, tried to be very careful not to do your own gaslighting by presenting the other parent as "bad".

This is one of the primary reasons for the writing of this book. Children are quite vulnerable, have had little experience, and are dependent on their parents for so much. If this book helps even a few children and parents, I will consider it a success. And I would suggest that you make good use of professional advice in approaching this topic.

THE IMPACT ON CHILDREN LIVING WITH A PARENT WHO SUFFERS FROM NPD

THIS IS A **VERY SERIOUS DIMENSION** TO AND CRUCIAL ASPECT WHICH CAN AND SHOULD BE CONSIDERED BY ANYONE CO PARENTING WITH SOMEONE WHO HAS NPD, especially if you are in the process of deciding to continue or discontinue the relationship.

As stated in many ways above, and NPD affected person has such an extreme level of self-involvement that they are most often incapable of empathy, compassion, or the ability to see their children as separate beings from themselves. This same person will almost always see themselves as "victims". They are not aware of the real reasons when they're all suffering. The blame is almost 100% projected out to someone/ in their disordered worlds. Most commonly that will be the other parent. Everyone affected by NPD lives a life of continued and painful distress. Children most often have a very real and instinctual awareness when one of their parents is in distress. Almost always their response is to try to relieve the pain they see their parent in.

While this is true of almost all children, those born to NPD parents will not have the knowledge or sophistication to understand the cause of this distress. They will inevitably make every attempt they can to support that parent and try to relieve this stress. The result in children is an acceptance of the delusion as real; acceptance of the demonization as real and valid; absolute alignment with the disordered parent in their expressed belief; no recognition of difference between objective reality and the delusional belief (including false allegations); and no sense of injustice.

However, when the distress is a result of internal disorder, children, especially young children, will be unable to determine the difference between the parent's projection of their own disorder and reality. When a parent is so disordered that their behavior destroys a marriage, that parent is often in a lot of emotional distress. Remember that the core of narcissism is a pathological terror.

It is generally heartwarming to see a child being supportive of a distressed parent. Yes, in this situation, the children will be drawn into aligning themselves with the world of the disordered parent. Added to that, is that those parents need to seek and obtain all the narcissistic supplies that they need. That puts the children in the position of accepting the projections of the disordered parent.

The results of the above are many. In a relationship that is ongoing, the children will inevitably be alienated from the healthy apparent. The result in children is an acceptance of the delusion as real; acceptance of the demonization as real and valid; absolute alignment with the disordered parent in their expressed belief; no recognition of difference between objective reality and the delusional belief (including false allegations); and no sense of injustice.

That is obviously damaging. In a relationship that is disintegrating, the children will be put in a position of having to choose one parent over the other. This may be a bigger dilemma than anticipated. The parent with NPD will be unable to see the damage being caused to the children because of their own inability to empathize and their own need for continued and ongoing narcissistic supply. The parent without NPD will see their children being alienated from but will only have the choice to join the alienation dynamics of the other parent or lose the children's bond with them. There is really no good choice in this situation. Either you relinquish the affections of your children to an unhealthy parent or you put them in the position of failing to support the parent they see as in distress.

My strongest suggestion is offered to these parents: DO NOT RATIONALIZE or IGNORE THE "RED FLAGS!" GET A LOT OF SUPPORT, RELIABLE GUIDANCE, AND VALID PSYCHOLOGICAL INPUT.

The result in children is an acceptance of the delusion as real; acceptance of the demonization as real and valid; absolute alignment with the disordered parent in their expressed belief; no recognition of difference between objective reality and the delusional belief (including false allegations); and no sense of injustice.

In contrast, an adult subjected to this treatment develops confusion; a recognition of contradiction between the delusion vs. observable reality; feelings of hurt; feelings of injustice; anger; and sometime pity toward the disordered person. But an adult subjected to these forces will not become an alienated adult, because an adult has sufficient independent perspective and a developed personality to maintain their own understanding and beliefs.

In effect, a healthy adult is pushed away from the delusion; while children are drawn into it and completely assimilated into it. By their assimilation, they serve to stabilize the delusion for the disordered parent, and the children may become a proxy for the parent in asserting the delusion and demonizing challengers to it.

When a parent is so disordered that their behavior destroys a marriage, that parent is often in a lot of emotional distress. Remember that the core of both narcissism and borderline is a pathological terror.

With a psychologically disordered parent who appears weak or troubled, children will ally themselves psychologically with whatever their needy parent expresses, as a way of supporting and strengthening that parent.

When a parent is struggling, children will do their best to stabilize and support their weakened parent. It's not a reasoned, chosen plan, but rather something they are intrinsically motivated to do. It leads children to take responsibility, make choices, and act to support their parent in the best way they can.

When a parent is so disordered that their behavior destroys a marriage, that parent is often in a lot of emotional distress. Remember that the core of both narcissism and borderline is a pathological terror. Terror is sickening, and the thoughts underlying the terror - the faults in the parent's character and behavior - are depressing. It's not unusual for such parents to show the stress and depression they live with, and they often abuse alcohol and drugs too. Children see this, and they recognize, at some level, that their parent is struggling.

But with a psychologically disordered parent who appears weak or troubled, children will ally themselves psychologically with whatever their needy parent expresses, as a way of supporting and strengthening that parent.

The most common point seeing someone who is married to a disordered partner, is great distress yet not knowing what to do. Too often they lose track of themselves in the chaos and craziness of dealing with the unpredictable accusations and distortions thrown at them by a constantly angry partner. People with these disorders have a pathological terror that others will find less than perfect. Saying pathological terror, means real terror, so strong that extreme reactions result from the threat, or even perceived threat.

The most common characteristic seen in someone who is married to a disordered partner, is great distress yet not knowing what to do. Too often they lose track of themselves in the chaos and confusion of dealing with the unpredictable accusations and distortions thrown at them by a constantly angry partner.

The following list is a collection of some of the more commonly observed behaviors and traits of those who suffer from NPD. Note that these are intended to be used for diagnosis. People who suffer from NPD are all unique and so each person will display a different subset of traits. Also, note that everyone displays "narcissistic" behaviors from time to time. Therefore, if a person exhibits one or some of these traits that does not necessarily qualify them for diagnosis NPD.

See the DSM 5 2015

Criteria on this page are intended for diagnostic criteria.

1. <u>Abusive cycle</u> - this is the name for the ongoing rotation between destructive and construct he which is typical in many dysfunctional relationships and families;
2. <u>Alienation</u> - the act of cutting off and/ or interfering with an individual's relationships with others;
3. <u>"always and never"</u> statements - declarations containing the

words always whenever are commonly used but rarely true;

4. <u>Anger</u> - people who suffer from NPD often feel a sense of unresolved anger and a heightened or exaggerated perception that they have been wronged, invalidated, neglected or abused;

5. <u>Belittling, condescending</u> - this kind of speech is a passive-aggressive approach to giving someone for bold a bus this they say is a great had door run xxx

6. e of putdown while maintaining a façade of reasonableness or for a long for her or;

7. <u>Blaming</u> - the practice of identifying a person or people responsible for creating a problem, rather than identifying ways of dealing with the problem;

8. <u>Bullying</u> - any systematic action of hurting a person from a position of relative physical, social, economic or emotional strength;

9. <u>Cheating</u> - sharing a romantic or intimate relationship with somebody when you are already committed to a monogamous relationship with someone else;

10. <u>Chronic broken promises</u> - repeatedly making and then breaking commitments;

11. <u>Denial</u> - believing or imagining that some painful or traumatic circumstance, event or memory does not exist or did not happen;

12. ~~Dissociation~~ - a psychological term used to describe a mental departure from reality;

13.   <u>Domestic   theft   </u>- consuming or taking control of a resource or asset belonging to a family member, partner, or spouse without obtaining their approval;

14.   <u>Emotional abuse </u>- any pattern of behavior directed at one individual by another which promotes in them a destructive sense of fear, obligation, or guilt;

15.   <u>Emotional blackmail </u>- a system of threats and punishments used in an attempt to control someone's behaviors;

16.   <u>Gaslighting</u> - the practice of brainwashing or convincing a mentally healthy individual that they are going insane or that their understanding of reality is mistaken or false;

17. <u>Grooming-</u> is the predatory act of maneuvering another individual into a position that makes them more isolated, dependent, likely to trust and more vulnerable to abusive behavior;

18. <u>Harassment</u> - any sustained or chronic pattern of unwelcome behavior by one individual towards another;

19. <u>Hoovering</u> - a term that describes how an abuse victim tries to assert their own rights by limiting contact in a dysfunctional relationship, gets "sucked back in" when the perpetrator temporarily exhibits improved or desirable behavior;

20. <u>Imposed isolation</u> - when abuse results in a person becoming isolated from **their**

support network, including friends and family;

21.   <u>Impulsiveness</u> the tendency to act or speak based on current feelings rather than logical reasoning;

22.   <u>Intimidation</u> - the creation or promotion of an environment which encourages an individual to believe that their thoughts, beliefs, values, or physical presence are inferior, flawed, problematic or worthless;

23.   <u>Lack of conscience</u> - individuals who suffer from personality disorders are often preoccupied with their own agendas, often to the exclusion of the needs and concerns of others.

24.   <u>Emotional abuse</u> - any pattern of behavior directed toward one individual by

another which promotes in them a destructive sense of fear, obligation, or guilt;

25. <u>Emotional blackmail</u> - a system of threats and punishments used to control someone's behavior;

26. <u>False accusations</u> - patterns of unwarranted or exaggerated criticism directed toward someone else;

27. <u>Scapegoating;</u> - systematically giving a dysfunctional amount of negative treatment to one individual among a family or group of peers;

28. <u>Manipulation</u> - the practice of steering an individual into a desired behavior for achieving a hidden personal goal;

29. <u>Masking</u> - covering up one's own natural outward appearance, mannerisms and

speech in dramatic and inconsistent ways depending on the situation;

30. Narcissism - a set of behaviors characterized by a pattern of grandiosity, self-centered focus, and lack of empathy or consideration for others;

31. Neglect - a passive form of abuse in which the physical or emotional needs of a dependent are disregarded or ignored;

32. Normalizing - a tactic used to desensitize an individual to abuse, coercive or inappropriate behaviors. Normalizing is the manipulation of another human being to get them to agree to or accept something that conflicts with the law, social norms, or their own basic code of behavior;

33.   <u>Not my fault syndrome</u> - avoiding personal responsibility for one's own words and actions;

34.   <u>Objectification</u> - the practice of treating a person like an object;

35.   <u>Parental alienation syndrome</u> - when a separated parent convinces their child that the other parent is bad, evil, or worthless;

36.   <u>Pathological lying</u> - persistent deception by an individual to serve their own needs;

37.   <u>Shaming</u> - the difference between blaming and shaming is that in blaming someone tells you that you did something bad, in shaming someone tells you that you are something bad;

38.   <u>Stalking</u> - any pervasive or unwelcome pattern of pursuing unwelcome contact with another individual;

39.   <u>Targeted humor, mocking and sarcasm</u> - pattern of joking, sarcasm or mockery which is designed to reduce and others reputation in their own eyes or in the eyes of others;

40.   <u>Thought policing</u> - a process of trying to question, control, or unduly influence another person's thoughts or feelings;

41.   <u>Threats</u> - inappropriate, intentional warnings of destructive actions or consequences;

42.   <u>Triangulation</u> - giving an advantage over perceived rivals by manipulating them into conflicts with each other

43. <u>Raging, violence, and impulsive aggression</u> - explosive verbal, physical or emotional elevations of a dispute. Rages threaten the security or safety of another individual and violate their personal boundaries;

44. <u>Relationship hypervigilance</u> - maintaining an unhealthy level of interest in the behaviors, comments, thoughts, and interests of others;

45. Sabotage - the spontaneous disruption of calm or status quo in order to serve a personal interest, provoke a conflict or draw attention;

46. <u>Selective memory and selective amnesia</u> - the use of memory will lack of memory which is selective to the point

of reinforcing a bias, belief or desired outcome;

47.   <u>Self-aggrandizement</u> - a pattern of pompous behavior, boasting, narcissism or competitiveness designed to create an appearance of superiority;

48.   <u>Sense of entitlement</u> - an unrealistic, unmerited, or inappropriate expectation of favorable living conditions or treatment at the hands of others

Trump's conservative defenders are attempting something extraordinary: to politically normalize abnormal psychology. Their sycophancy enables a sickness.

ABUSIVE BEHAVIOR IS PERVASIVE AND WITHOUT AWARENESS, IT WILL CONTINUE.

SEVEN MAJOR TYPES OF ABUSE:

PHYSICAL ABUSE IS INTIMIDATION, ISOLATION, RESTRAINT, AGGRESSION AND ENDANGERMENT;

MENTAL ABUSE IS GASLIGHTING, SILENCE, MANIPULATION AND VICTIMIZATION;

VERBAL ABUSE IS SCREAMING, BULLYING,

By Mayo Clinic Staff

Narcissistic personality disorder is one of several types of personality disorders. Personality disorders are conditions in which people have traits that cause them to feel and behave in socially distressing ways, limiting their ability to function in relationships and other areas of their life, such as work or school.

If you have narcissistic personality disorder, you may come across as conceited, boastful or pretentious. You often monopolize conversations. You may belittle or look down on people you perceive as inferior. You may feel a sense of entitlement — and when you don't receive special treatment, you may become impatient or angry. You may insist on having "the best" of everything — for instance, the best car, athletic club or medical care.

At the same time, you have trouble handling anything that may be perceived as criticism. You may have secret feelings of insecurity, shame, vulnerability and humiliation. To feel better, you may react with rage or contempt and try to belittle the other person to make yourself appear superior. Or you may feel depressed and moody because you fall short of perfection.

Many experts use the criteria in the Diagnostic and Statistical Manual of Mental Disorders (DSM-5), published by the American Psychiatric Association, to diagnose mental conditions. This manual is also used by insurance companies to reimburse for treatment.

DSM-5 criteria for narcissistic personality disorder include these features:

- Having an exaggerated sense of self-importance
- Expecting to be recognized as superior even without achievements that warrant it
- Exaggerating your achievements and talents

- Being preoccupied with fantasies about success, power, brilliance, beauty or the perfect mate
- Believing that you are superior and can only be understood by or associate with equally <u>special people</u>
- Requiring constant admiration
- Having a sense of entitlement
- Expecting special favors and unquestioning compliance with your expectations
- Taking advantage of others to get what you want
- Having an inability or unwillingness to recognize the needs and feelings of others
- Being envious of others and believing others envy you
- Behaving in an arrogant or haughty manner

Although some features of narcissistic personality disorder may seem like having confidence, it's not the same. Narcissistic personality disorder crosses the border of healthy confidence into thinking so highly of yourself that you put yourself on a <u>pedestal </u>and value yourself above others.

When you have narcissistic personality disorder, you may not want to think that anything could be wrong — doing so wouldn't fit with your NEED for a self-image of power and perfection. People with narcissistic personality disorder are most likely to seek treatment when they become depressed, often because of perceived criticisms or rejections.